Illustrated **BUYER'S ★ GUIDE**™

MODERN
SPORTS
& GT CARS
Under $20K

Matt Stone

MBI Publishing Company

First published in 2001 by MBI Publishing Company, Galtier Plaza, Suite 200, 380 Jackson Street, St. Paul, MN 55101-3885 USA

MBI Publishing Company books are also available at discounts in bulk quantity for industrial or sales-promotional use. For details write to Special Sales Manager at Motorbooks International Wholesalers & Distributors, Galtier Plaza, Suite 200, 380 Jackson Street, St. Paul, MN 55101-3885 USA

Library of Congress Cataloging-in-Publication Data
Stone, Matthew L.
    Modern sports & GT cars under $20k / Matt Stone.
        p.cm. -- (Illustrated buyer's guide)
    Includes index.
    ISBN 0-7603-0899-3 (pbk. : alk. paper)
        1. Sports cars--Purchasing. I. Title: Modern sports and GT cars under $20k. II Title. III. Motorbooks International illustrated buyers guide series

TL162.S76 2001
629.222'1'0296--dc21

On the front cover: Who would've guessed that any one of these great sports cars could be had for under 20 grand? Noted automotive photographer David Newhardt captured three of the 1990s' hottest sports and GT cars for the cover: the Toyota Supra Turbo, Mazda RX-7 R2, and Nissan 300ZX Turbo. How hot are these cars? The combined power output of this trio is 855 horsepower. *David Newhardt*

On the title page: Nobody will every accuse the BMW E30 M3 as being anything but a thinly disguised race car. Subtlety was just not part of the deal. This bird's-eye view demonstrates the shape and width of the fenders' blister-style flares that are required primarily for the racing version. *BMW*

On the back cover: Miata owners seem to continually debate whether the earliest 1.6-liter cars, the later 1.8-liter models, or the second generation 1999 and later Miatas are really the pinnacle of Mazda's best-selling sports car. It doesn't matter; they're all a great value for someone who desires pure, wind-in-your-hair sports car fun. *Ron Perry, courtesy of Mazda*

Edited by John Adams-Graf
Designed by Bruce Leckie

Printed in United States of America

Contents

Acknowledgments

No project of this nature happens in a vacuum; there are many people whom I thank for their assistance. They are:

Tim Parker, Zack Miller, and my editor for this project, John Adams-Graf, all of MBI Publishing

Editor-in-Chief C. Van Tune, and the rest of my colleagues at *Motor Trend,* especially David Newhardt, who provided many photographs for this effort

The members of the Motor Press Guild

Freelance photographer pal Jim Brown

Kevin and Dawn Coughlin, for the use of their Alfa Spider

Debi Mead, Dan Barnes, and Matt Wiggins

My appreciation as well to the many manufacturer public/media relations professionals who supplied photographs and/or product information, including:

Lisa Barrow, DaimlerChrysler Public Relations

Rob Mitchell and Dave Butchko, BMW North America

Brian Betz, formerly of Mazda North American Operations

Fred Aikins, Mazda North American Operations

Nancy Libby and Patty Garcia, GM Communications

Alicia Smith, Honda Public Relations

Ming-Jou Chen, Toyota Product News

Bob Carlson and Eleanor Smith, Porsche Cars of North America

Harold Allen and Sandra Badgett, Ford Public Affairs

Scott Vazin and Kurt Von Zumwalt, Nissan Public Affairs

Mike Spencer and Matt Pearson, Acura Public Affairs

A special thanks to my family for putting up with my doing yet another book project, and lastly to *you.* You reached into your pocket and pulled out your hard-earned bucks (or your well-worn credit card) to buy this book. Had you not, I'd have had no reason to write it. Thanks again, and when you're done reading, I hope you feel you got, or saved, your money's worth—a hundred times over.

Introduction

Admit it: Ferrari's 360 Modena is one of the most spectacular automobiles that came along in Y2K. It sprints to 60 in around four seconds, tops out near 180, and its metallurgy rivals that of the space shuttle. You'd buy one in a minute—and so would I—if it weren't for the fact that it would set us each back about a hundred fifty grand. Bummer . . .

Still, the twentieth century's final decade produced some impressive machinery: cars that would indeed outperform the Ferraris of not too many years previous. Increased use of computer-aided design, and revolutions in automotive electronics, engine management systems, and tire technology begot cars that were ever more reliable, economical, and more fun to drive—all at the same time.

This book is intended to be a hands-on primer to selecting affordable, sporting wheels that you can drive every day. We won't be shy about pointing out particular models that are more—or less—desirable than others. The "everyday" factor is important, hence our focus on newer hardware. Yes, there are boatloads of desirable automobiles from the 1950s and 1960s that everyone lusts over. But "classics" are something altogether different. Few *really* make practical, everyday transport. Example: I own a 1966 Sunbeam Tiger, a little British convertible powered by a Ford V-8 engine. It has no power steering, no radio, no cup holders, no air bags, no air conditioning, and no place to plug in a cell phone. CD player? Forget it. Power windows/doors/locks and a tilt wheel? Wrong era. You can't lock the doors, the top leaks, and it needs a good old-fashioned tune-up every 5,000–6,000 miles. Great weekend toy? For sure. Drive it/park it/leave it anywhere transportation? You gotta be kidding.

Automotive designers, executives, and journalists have been trying to define the term "sports car" ever since Stutz built the first Bearcat in the 1920s. Purists would insist that a genuine sports car has rear-wheel drive, seats only two people, and has a top that goes down or comes off. Or maybe no top at all. We understand that mindset, but again, not exactly practical.

For the sake of this Buyer's Guide, we've also included cars with front-wheel drive, four seats, and/or a permanent metal top—though they still must have a maximum of two doors (hmmmm . . . *Sports Sedans Under $20K* might also be an interesting subject for another Buyer's Guide). The main requirement for inclusion is that each must offer some combination of performance and style, plus be affordable to the common man or woman. If they don't or aren't, they're not discussed here. More often than not, we address only—or at least primarily—the top-performance offering for any given model. We feel that if you took the effort to buy this book, you are an enthusiast to some degree, and interested in sports car levels of performance and handling. So we stuck to the hotter variants, though not every car in here is a high-buck piece.

As mentioned, this is a primer, a reference for you to get to know a wide variety of cars. Some cars, such as the Mazda Miata and Nissan 300ZX, were offered in so many models and variants that we can't hope to catalog and discuss them all in this rather limited amount of space. So this book should by no means represent your only homework—it's really just the place to start.

Why $20K and under? Seemed like a good number to us, if for no other reason than there are darn few exciting sports and GT cars available new for less than that amount. Some of the newer, pricier models reviewed herein will edge right up to that $20,000 ceiling, or in fact may still be above it. But very few of these cars are sought-after classics that are likely to appreciate to any great degree. So those that are still more money (as of this writing) will likely fall below the $20K level at some point in the future. Others are readily available for a fourth of that.

Besides, if money didn't matter, you'd be down at the Ferrari dealership, right?

Tips On Shopping, Test Driving, and Buying

Cars are where you find them. Especially used cars. A common question is, "What's the best way to find a good used car?" The answer: whatever way actually helps you locate the *right* car. Private party? Local paper? Used car dealers? New car dealers? The Internet? Telling your friends? The local "lemon lot"? I say use the old standby, multiple-choice test answer: E) All of the above. Why limit yourself? Use any combination of these methods to look at a reasonable number of vehicles so you can make an informed purchase. But deciding what you want, and then how best to find it, are only part of the deal.

Choosing a vehicle means establishing a matrix of the following:

- Needs (How you drive, where you drive, how many people you carry)
- Budget (How much you've saved and/or can comfortably borrow)
- Emotion (What you want, and what will make you happy)

Is a car just transportation to you, or are you trying to make a statement about yourself? Are you a performance-oriented driver, or just want cool wheels? How important are operating costs, reliability, and the like? Can you perform certain maintenance and upkeep procedures yourself, or do you depend on dealers and independent shops for car care?

For some, any one of several cars will make them happy; others insist on trying to find a used car that meets their exact specifications, as if you could actually still order one new. I can't tell you where you fit on these scales; just know that everyone is different, and you should be aware of how your wants, needs, and budget play into the purchase process. Once it's time to go out and look at a vehicle, there are several steps you can take to mitigate your risk and zero in on the right car for you.

After you've read this book, but before you test drive, arm yourself with price, model, and technical information. Use the Web to determine current estimated retail and wholesale values for the vehicle in question. Check your local newspaper to see if any similar models are for sale, and for how much. If applicable, call a dealer and ask what this make and model should be worth. Pricing information is now readily available, and it's one of those cases where "Knowledge is Power." Two particularly

The best place to find an affordable sports car deal is where you find it! When you are ready to buy, any source is a good one. Newspapers, car clubs, the Internet, and word of mouth are all great ways to find a car. This relatively rare Toyota MR2 was spotted while out driving.

While most of us would love to have a new Ferrari or Porsche, it is amazing how much fun an affordable sports car can be. Just identify your requirements, prioritize the features and characteristics that you want in a car, and identify which models fit the bill. Then do your research and go shopping!*Ron Perry, courtesy of Mazda*

Keep a notebook and pencil in your car. When you see a "For Sale" sign on a car you are interested in, like this clean Dodge Stealth, stop and check it out. Write down notes about the car, where and when you saw it, and, of course, the seller's phone number.

good sources are Kelly Blue Book (www.kbb.com) and Edmunds Price Guide (www.edmunds.com). Either will allow you to enter the vehicle's year, make, model, equipment, and condition, and give you typical, up-to-date retail and wholesale pricing.

While you're online, see what you can find out about this particular make and model. Several websites give owner-satisfaction information, as well as quality ratings and recall notifications. Most of the more popular models have spawned enthusiast websites dedicated specifically to them. Some are small, personal sites that tell you about one person's car and experiences, while others are huge repositories of information and parts/service/modification resources. I've included a number of URLs that I found while assembling this book, and there are new ones going live every day. As with all websites, information quality varies. But it's never been easier to have a ton of it to review.

I'm a strong believer in the value of enthusiast owners' clubs. Whether you choose to never attend a meeting, or want to become club president, *nobody* knows more about the ins and outs of any car than the clubbies. Join the club (every marque seems to have one, some have several), check out its website, and ask members for the dos and don'ts of the model you want. Many offer classifieds and car-locating services

too, which may help you get an inside deal on a club member's car for sale.

No matter whether the car you're looking at is being offered at a dealership, by a private party, or via the Web, get as much detailed information on its history as you can. How many owners has it had? Is the odometer mileage correct? Has it ever been in any minor—or major—accidents? What service records are available? What major components have been replaced, and what is currently in need of repair? Is there any factory warranty remaining? In the case of a private owner, find out why they're selling it. The goal here is to help you determine if the car has had a normal, reasonably well-maintained life, or if it's really on its last leg.

A proper test drive is critical. Here's my checklist for doing it right:

- Never perform a first test drive at night. All cars seem to look better in the dark and run better in cool weather. If you have to, visit the car again during daylight hours before buying it.
- Before you hop in, look over the car for accident damage: mismatched paint, poor panel fit, sagging doors, etc. (More about accident damage in a moment.)
- Before starting the engine, check the oil, radiator coolant, transmission fluid (if possible), brake

fluid, etc. Are these lifebloods clean and fresh looking, or worse than last week's coffee?

- Check underneath the car for leaks.
- If at all possible, start up the engine from cold. This will give you an opportunity to see if it's making any expensive rattles or emitting any smoke or other fumes. A cold-start is the best time to identify any of these problems, as most go away—or at least quiet down—when the car is warm.
- While the engine is warming up, adjust the seat and mirrors to determine if you'll be comfortable in this particular model.
- Select a test-drive route that encompasses a variety of conditions: freeway, stop and go, rough road, curvy stretches, and the like.
- Your route should also be at *least* five miles long— 10 is better yet. If the owner insists on "just around the block," then he's probably hiding something.
- Look and listen: are there strange noises, a rough ride, a jerky clutch, or grabbing brakes? Does the car pull to the left? The need for mechanical repairs may not cross a car off your list. But it should at least raise the questions, "What is the problem, and how much will it cost to fix?" Make a list of anything you are not sure about, and discuss it with the owner/dealer before you begin negotiating on the price of the car. While you don't want to appear to be picking apart the car, the owner needs to know you are aware of these problems, and they could become a positive negotiating point in your favor. This aspect of evaluating a prospective purchase is critical— take it from a guy who's bought and sold more than 100 cars.

If this first test drive goes well, I recommend you have the car inspected by a qualified mechanic. Even if you are pretty sharp mechanically, putting the car up on a lift and having it checked over using today's sophisticated diagnostic equipment can tell you a lot. This service can be performed by a dealer or an independent who works on this particular brand. Plan on spending anywhere from $75 to $200; this is your cost, not the seller's, but if it reveals a major problem, it could save you a fortune.

Having an independent inspection performed is probably more important when looking at a private party car than when shopping at a dealer. Dealers generally offer most late-model used cars with some sort of warranty, or will make certain repairs as part of the purchase contract. They may have also performed some reconditioning work before the car went on the lot—though not always, so ask. Not every dealer in the world is reputable and ethical, but quite a few are; going back to deal with them on problem issues is often easier than trying to establish recourse with a private owner. Private sales are generally considered "as is, as seen"—though the price will usually be less.

With a private party, the owner may not even know of an impending problem. But if they refuse to let you take the vehicle to the shop of your choice for an inspection, again they're probably hiding something. Most mechanical issues can be repaired in such a way that the car can be made as good as new, save one: major accident damage. In the old days, cars had frames that were separate from their bodies. That means a dented fender could be unbolted and replaced easily, possibly having had no negative effect on the vehicle's frame structure. The overwhelming majority of today's cars employ their body panels and a series of other metal stampings to create the car's structure (called a "unitbody," or "monocoque"); there is no separate frame. That means if a car takes a hard enough hit, the *entire structure* can be knocked out of alignment. This damage can be fixed too, but it's very difficult to completely realign every aspect of the structure to where it's *perfectly factory true* again. Doors may not fit, trunks don't close, and the car may steer differently depending on whether you're turning left or right. Not good.

Although there are always exceptions, it's my recommendation that if you can determine the subject vehicle has had major bodywork (i.e., more than one body panel replaced, or any manner of chassis straightening or alignment), it's best to *walk away*, no matter how good the rest of the deal might seem. Few models discussed in this book are so rare and valuable that you won't ever find another one, so it's seldom worth buying one that is irreparably tweaked. Even if the new paint looks shiny and the car seems to drive well enough, no body shop can replicate the structural integrity built in at the factory, so a car that's incurred major damage will never be quite right.

For many areas of the country, rust is almost as imposing a specter as accident damage. Today's cars are built with more effective rust prevention technology than ever before. And many manufacturers even warren against outer-body rust-through. Still, the tinworm is something to keep an eye out for. The most important thing to remember about rust is that it's easy to prevent before it starts, and difficult to stop once it does. Rust attacks a car in two ways: cosmetically and structurally. Both involve oxidation of the

Some cars, like this Mustang GT (above), are readily available. Others, like this Nissan 240SX (below), are less common. But you never know when or where the "perfect" car will come along, so either one is worth a look.

metal, but it's important to understand the difference. Cosmetic rust is just what it sounds like; visible, but doesn't affect the physical structure of the vehicle. It's not pretty, but probably doesn't make the car unsafe. Rust that's found its way to structural parts of the car, particularly the engine mounts, suspension mounting points, shock-absorber and muffler brackets, and the like, can be expensive to repair and may even make the

car unsafe. As noted, we're dealing with ten-year-or-less-old iron here, benefiting the latest rustproofing coatings and processes—yet have still seen seven-year-old cars with structural rust bad enough that we wouldn't buy or recommend them. So, if you live in a area that salts its roads and rusts out cars, ask the owner if the undercarriage was washed out regularly, or had any other rust-prevention measures taken. If not, get the car to a professional who can put it up on a hoist, and check it out thoroughly. Then, negotiate for any required repairs, or consider another car if the situation is bad enough.

Negotiation style is a very personal thing. Some folks love to haggle; others are scared to death to ask a seller to take a penny less than their asking price. Entire books have been written on the art of negotiation, so we won't get into it here. Just be armed with the aforementioned price information, and know that more than 90 percent of private sellers do indeed accept something less than their original asking price. What about dealers? The number who bargain—at least a little—is probably closer to 100 percent. And remember, it matters little where you start: it's the final price that has to feel right to both of you.

Performance modifications are a double-edged sword: done well, they can enhance a vehicle's appeal and performance, and perhaps increase its price. Done poorly, they can actually *reduce* its performance—and its value. Another problem is that the owner may attempt to price the vehicle based on what he has invested in it, not by what it's really worth on the open market in its modified state. Don't pay extra for a vehicle that has hardware on it that you don't like or is of low quality. You're almost always better off buying a well-maintained original that hasn't been driven hard, and adding high-quality performance parts if you wish. So gauge the value, benefit, and appeal of performance modifications carefully, based on what you really want.

The only detail remaining is vehicle transfer paperwork. The vast majority of dealerships can take care of all the paperwork on site—this includes the transfer of title, licensing as required, and emissions certifications. But a little extra care is advised when dealing with a private party. I suggest you meet your seller at the DMV office or AAA branch to do the transfer. He'll need to bring the vehicle, the registration, certificate of ownership, and possibly the license plates (if turn-in is required). The main reason for doing it all at a neutral and official location is that the DMV (or AAA, which has full access to the DMV database) can make sure the paperwork—most particularly the VIN, or Vehicle Identification Number—matches the vehicle for sale, and that there are no outstanding liens or warrants against your new toy. Time is littered with examples of someone handing a certified check, or even cash, over to the seller, then driving off with paperwork for a vehicle other than the one he thought he bought. That "seller," of course, was really a thief—who now has your money for what may have been a stolen car to begin with. And the burden of proof is on you—if the police can catch him.

When dealing with a private party, it's quite possible that you'll be looking at a car that has an outstanding loan balance. Depending on the rate, terms, and your bank balance, it might be beneficial to assume this loan; new car rates and terms are generally better on those available for used cars, and if you're buying from the person who bought it new, the loan terms could be more attractive than you could get. However, you must check with the lender to determine if the loan can be properly assumed—don't just take the payment book and start writing checks. More often than not, the loan will need to be paid off, and that lender is holding the certificate of ownership. You and the seller must check with the lender, determine how they will accept payment for the vehicle, and what procedures are required to get the lien released, and a new title sent to you (or you and your new lender). Finally, make sure to keep a copy of the seller's lender information and loan number, in case documents get held up, and you need to do some follow-up to ensure the transaction is complete. Moral: Make sure it all matches, and effect a proper transfer with no loose ends.

Now, crank up the stereo, and head for your favorite highway.

REPORT CARD	
Engine	A-/A+
Transmission	B+
Power/Weight Ratio	B+/A-
Handling	A-/A+
Braking	A-/A+
Ride	B-
Exterior Styling	B-/B
Interior Styling	B+
Interior Function	B+
Cargo Capacity	B
Everyday Usability	B/C
Reliability	A
Fit and Finish	A
Market Availability	A/C
Resale Value Potential	B-/A-
Fun Factor	B/A
Bang for Buck	A-
Aftermarket Interest	A+
Club Support	A

Acura Integra GS-R/Type R (1994–1999)

Honda's normal product cycle, that is, the number of years a particular model stays around before it's remodeled or replaced, is four years. The fact that the current, third-generation Integra has been around for twice that (eight model years as of this writing) is testimony to its basic goodness as a design, and popularity in the marketplace.

When launched in 1994, its four-small-headlights front end was controversial, yet as time has gone on, more and more makers have actually returned to some sort of round headlamp look. The Integra two-door was initially offered in RS and LS trim, as well as the higher performance, VTEC-engined GS-R. The top performance version is the high-revving, limited-production Type R. We'll focus on the latter two models, as they are the sportiest versions with the most performance potential.

This 1996 GS-R demonstrates what may be the most controversial aspect of the Integra's styling: those four small round headlights. However, more and more cars are returning to this look these days, perhaps one of the reasons the Integra has remained a popular seller in this market segment for eight model years (1994–2001). *Acura*

The rear aspect of this 1994 demonstrates the Integra's basic wedge shape. This rear wing is standard on GS-R models. This wheel is the 1994/1995 GS-R design. *Acura*

What really sets the GS-R apart from the more pedestrian Integras is its 1.8-liter, DOHC, 170-horsepower "VTEC" four. What gives this engine so much extra power, as compared to the equally sized 142-horse four found in GS/LS Integras, is its variable valve timing system, which Honda calls VTEC. VTEC electromechanically switches between standard and more aggressive cam profiles at 4,400 rpm; this system manages both the intake and exhaust side of the engine, and the change in the engine's attitude is dramatic, right on up to its 8,000-rpm redline. VTEC is effective (you'll also read about it with reference to many Honda models), as there are many turbocharged four and V-6 engines that don't put out any more power than this. The GS-R was offered only with a close ratio five-speed manual transmission.

The Integra packs GT-worthy hardware to make the most of the VTEC powerplant. That means a fully

Very little had changed by 1998, this being that year's GS-R; note the fresh alloy wheel design. *Acura*

The real go-er of the Integra lineup—the Type R. 1997 was the first year for this limited-edition model, and it's easily distinguished by the monochrome paint job that even extends to the wheels. *Acura*

independent suspension, featuring upper and lower A-arms at the front, instead of the more common—and less expensive—MacPherson struts. This A-arm setup lets the suspension maintain more constant caster and camber attitudes during cornering. Steering is via a power, variable-ratio rack-and-pinion setup, and Honda equipped the GS-R with four-wheel disc brakes (vented up front) with standard ABS.

The interior design is handsome and straightforward, devoid of gimmicks. A sculptured central binnacle houses the main gauges, which are easy to see and read. A center console holds the HVAC and sound systems, the only fly in the ergonomic ointment being slide controls for the fan and temp controls instead of easy-to-use twist knobs. Dual air bags were standard, as was a power moonroof, power windows/locks/mirrors, a tilt steering wheel, and an AM/FM/cassette stereo. It's a comfortable cabin, though not particularly long on rear-seat room, as is the case with most compact coupes. And it's a hatchback, which some still prefer over a more conventional trunk.

Since the Integra GS-R was all new in 1994, and instantly became the segment's top seller, there were few changes for 1995. Mechanical specs remained the same, though an optional leather-trimmed interior was offered for the first time. 1996 was another carryover year, save for newly styled alloy wheels. 1997 brought more of the same, at least for the GS-R; the only changes of note were the addition of a standard AM/FM/CD stereo unit, the bolstering of the side impact beams in order to meet tougher crash protection requirements, and a different wheel finish. The big news for 1997, however, was the introduction of the limited-edition, even-higher performance Type R.

Honda was quite successful as a builder of Formula One racing engines during the early 1990s, and finished the decade as a winning engine provider for the Championship Auto Racing Teams series as well. A bit of this high-revving engine tech trickled its way into production models in the form of the Acura's midengined exotic, the NSX, and the Integra Type R. A lighter valvetrain and pistons, a revised exhaust system, high-performance camshafts, special head work, and several other race-inspired engine mods increased the 1.8's horsepower rating to 195, and its redline to an even loftier 8,500 revs. The R's ride height was dropped by 15 millimeters to achieve a lower center of gravity, and the suspension's bushings, shock absorbers, anti-roll bars, and springs were re-tuned for even more aggressive handling. Brake discs were enlarged, and the Type R carries unique five-bolt wheels and hubs. Certain body stampings were thicker than the lesser Integras, which, along with front and rear chassis-stiffening bars, made for a more rigid structure. Visually, it is differentiated by a special rear wing and Type R identification. Most came without air conditioning, and other nonessential hardware (sunroof, vanity mirrors, cruise control, and some sound-deadening components and materials) was eliminated in the name of weight savings. Just 500 Type Rs were sold in North America for 1997.

Nineteen ninety-eight brought a few modifications to all Integras, in the form of restyled front and rear fascias and new parking, turn, and stoplight lenses. The Type R made a midyear return, and enjoyed the same changes, while the GS-R received yet another new wheel design, and color choices were shuffled.

The Type R went on hiatus for 1999 (although it was offered again for 2000), and as the Integra had been on the market for some years, equipment levels were adjusted to increase its value. The most notable change for the GS-R is the inclusion of leather upholstery as standard.

Integras tend to be reliable, trouble-free cars if given a modicum of care. Considering their high-revving nature (especially the Type R), frequent oil and filter changes are even more critical than they are with many other cars. Both the GS-R and Type R engines should go 100,000 miles without major repair, though stick to the factory-recommended intervals for cam/timing belt changes. Exhaust systems tend to fail near the 100,000-mile mark.

The manual transmissions are sturdy as well, though second-gear synchros could need attention as early as 75,000 miles if abused; the same goes for the clutch. The electrical systems are generally ultrareliable. The leather upholstery should wear well if conditioned, but the cloth interior doesn't hold up as well to sun and wear. Otherwise, there are few foibles to mention on these well-sorted, reliable sport coupes. The Type R is obviously the hot pick, but it's important to seek out a well-maintained, low-mileage

An interesting aspect of the Type R is that it offers up impressive handling and grip numbers on 15-inch wheels—sort of makes one wonder why so many Integra fans fit oversized 17- and 18-inchers. The answer is style, but the message is that the ultralow-profile rubber doesn't necessarily make a car handle better. *Acura*

The fact that the Integra GS-R's engine could remain on the market virtually unchanged for more than six model years is strong testimony to the excellence of its original design. As with most Honda engines, it's powerful for its size, relatively smooth, a bit soft on torque down low, but offers impressive power in the higher-rpm ranges. Sophisticated VTEC valve timing hardware has proven to be quite reliable over the years, but regular oil changes, and timing belt changes when called for, are mandatory. *Acura*

example. The reason is that the engine uses many Type R–specific parts, is virtually hand-built, and will prove very expensive to overhaul when the time comes. So a high-mile car can turn into a money pit.

Engaging to drive, reliable, practical for everyday use, and supported by an exceptionally vibrant aftermarket, the Integra GS-R is a still-modern sports coupe that ranks high in most areas. If you can find a good one, the Type R ranks as a serious performer, and even has a certain collector value—not so common for modern-day Japanese hardware.

The rear head/leg room in the Integra is just adequate, but this is a "singles/couples" kind of car anyway, so it's not a big issue. Thickly bolstered seats do an adequate job of holding occupants firm during hard cornering maneuvers, and materials are of typically high quality. Though not visible in this photo, we also like the way the gauges are easily visible through the steering wheel and easy to read, though items such as the HVAC control designs are not as good as is found on some of the newest machines. *Acura*

SPECIFICATIONS (1997 GS-R)

Body style . . . . Two door, five passenger
Drivetrain layout. . . . . Front engine, front drive
Engine type . . . . DOHC I-4
Displacement, liter/cc 1.8/1,797
Horsepower hp @ rpm, ... SAE net 170 @ 7,600
Torque, ft-lb @ rpm . . . . SAE net 128 @ 6,200
Transmission . . . . 5-speed manual
Wheelbase, in. 101.2
Length, in. 172.4
Width, in. 67.3
Height, in. 52.6
Base curb weight lb 2,667
Suspension, f/r . . . . Upper and lower A-arms/upper and lower A-arms
Steering type. . . . . Rack and pinion
Brakes, f/r. . . . . Disc/disc

PERFORMANCE

Acceleration, 0–60 mph . . . . 7.6 sec.
Standing quarter
mile, sec/mph 15.8/90.0
Source . . . . Road & Track

TYPICAL PARTS/REPAIR PRICES

Major tune-up/service. $330
Air filter 23
Shock absorber 86
Catalytic converter(s) 128
Clutch replacement 1,200

WEBSITES

honda-acura.net
acuraclub.com

REPORT CARD

Engine	C+
Transmission	B
Power/Weight Ratio	C+
Handling	C+
Braking	B
Ride	B+
Exterior Styling	A
Interior Styling	B
Interior Function	C+
Cargo Capacity	B
Everyday Usability	C+
Reliability	C
Fit and Finish	B-
Market Availability	C
Resale Value Potential	B+
Fun Factor	B
Bang for Buck	B
Aftermarket Interest	A-
Club Support	A

Alfa Romeo Spider (1991–1993)

The Alfa Spider holds several unique distinctions. First, it's (sadly) the only Italian car referenced in this book; had we been doing this project 30 years ago, there would have been all manner of Fiat, Lancia, and certainly other Alfa models to be discussed. Secondly, it's not a modern-day *representation* of a classic 1960s sports car—it is a *direct descendant* of a classic 1960s sports car; a "new old car," so to speak. And finally, it's one of the rarer finds discussed here, certainly when compared to Eclipse Spyders and GTIs. What other car discussed herein can brag about having worm and roller steering?

You can clearly see where these "Series 4" Spiders came from by looking at the original Alfa Duetto "roundtail" Spiders of the mid-1960s; the architecture of the Spider's powertrain traces back even further. This handsome Italian sportster was always a popular element of the Alfa lineup, and was updated every few years during the 1970s and 1980s, and again for the final time for 1991–1993 (hence the unofficial "Series 4" designation). Sadly, Alfa left the U.S. market altogether just a year later.

The Spider, whose classic lines were penned by Italian design house Pininfarina (also responsible for styling most of the Ferraris built over the last 40 years or so), was offered just one way: a two-seat convertible. Notable calling cards include its 2.0-liter; DOHC four (which has been built and sold in many sizes over the years, and also served as a more-than-successful racing powerplant); modern double-wishbone front suspension; antiquated live-axle rear suspension; four-wheel disc brakes; and a five-speed manual transmission, the shifter for which seems to sprout more from the dash than it does from the floor. Two models were offered: the standard Spider and the Spider Veloce. Both are identical mechanically and from a performance standpoint, but the Veloce has standard 15-inch alloy wheels (as opposed to the base Spider's steel units), air conditioning, and leather-trimmed interior.

By the time of its final updating for 1991, the Spider had become more of a luxury GT than a hard-edged sports car. Pininfarina deftly styled new, more modern-looking body-colored bumpers front and rear; revised taillights; and formed a subtle aerodynamic lip into the rear decklid, which replaced the more aggressive, though not nearly as harmonious-looking

Although the Alfa Romeo Spider Veloce's style dates back to the mid-1960s, it demonstrates that well-proportioned shapes can last. Those five-miles-per-hour bumpers weren't even a bad dream back when the original Duetto was designed, but Alfa had integrated them pretty well by the time of this 1991–1993 redesign.

Much the same can be said of the rear, as modern wraparound taillights and safety bumpers fit nicely onto a car that was never intended to have them. Tonneau neatly hides convertible top.

black rear spoiler on the previous- generation model. The interior was reconfigured to include a driver side air bag and other safety-related hardware; the leather or leather/cloth combination seats as found on the Veloce are both supportive and more luxurious than seen on previous models. You certainly wouldn't have seen air conditioning or power windows on a 1966 Duetto Spider, but as mentioned, the car's mission had changed over the years.

Driving a Spider today yields a distinctly vintage feel—classic, yet somehow reasonably modern (at least from an early 1990s standpoint). Unfortunately, time and the then-current state of emissions controls affairs were not particularly kind to the Alfa's classic engine design. While a 1960s or early 1970s Alfa is generally a high-revving, roarty sports car that served up a lot of driver feedback, at the expense of a smooth ride and quiet exhaust note, the latter-day Spider put out just 120 horsepower—compare that to something like the Honda S2000, which is good for exactly double that amount from an identically sized engine. While the Honda revs to 9,000 rpm, the Alfa starts to sound strained at about half that. Acceleration and cornering performance put it nearly on par with, or maybe just below, an early 1990s Miata. There was also an optional three-speed automatic transmission available, but it was an outdated unit even at the time, and did little to enhance the Spider's just-average performance—we'd recommend staying away from a Spider so-equipped.

But it's not all bad, to be sure. While the suspension doesn't serve up tons of grip, it does deliver a reasonably supple, polished ride, though the live rear axle

The shifter sprouts from the upper portion of the console, and takes a little getting used to, but is actually quite pleasant to operate once you get the hang of it. Lower dash knee protection is not a particularly handsome update, but was necessary by U.S. certification requirements, and at least gets the job done.

(Above and below) Optional removable hardtop is a rare piece, and in typical Italian fashion, is quite handsome. Alfa could have never guessed the Spider would have remained on the market for 27 years. *David Newhardt*

dances a bit on really rough pavement. The old-style steering provides reasonable road feel, and the brakes are clearly up to the job. Although the gearshift throws are on the longish side, and the unusual shifter location takes a little getting used to, the transmission has a wonderfully direct feel, much more satisfying than the cable shifter mechanisms found on so many front-drive cars. The top goes up and down relatively easily, though with a car like this, who wants to put the top up? There's also a rare, and thus somewhat expensive, removable hardtop available.

One of the reasons Alfa was flushed from our shores was an inability to deliver the quality control and reliability that car owners experienced with most German and Japanese carmakers, and had come to demand. The Alfa Spider is basically a well-engineered and robustly constructed car: major components such as the engine's internals, transmission, rear differential, and the frame/chassis are quite tough, and good for several hundred thousand miles when cared for.

It's the little things that a Spider owner will forever be chasing. The air conditioning system works well *when* it works, but seems to be quite frail. Any Italian car owner can tell you about constantly chasing electrical gremlins, though the severity of this problem seems to vary from car to car. Suspension bushings, of which there are many, don't seem particularly long-lived, and may need replacement as early as 75,000 miles. Interior materials—especially the abundance of leather—are handsome and luxurious, but can't handle the sun or bad weather. If the car you're looking at has the leather/cloth seat combo, chances are the cloth has either been replaced, or will need to be soon. The exhaust system, particularly the catalytic converter, is prone to failure and expensive to replace (though a nice aftermarket system will be good for a more enthusiastic exhaust note, and maybe a few additional horsepower as well). The fuel injection systems on earlier Spiders were problem-plagued, but we've heard few complaints with those found on these Series 4 cars.

Even though the Alfa Romeo marque, as well as the Spider itself, is well known for an impressive competition history, these last-series Spiders are cruisers, not racers. If you enjoy driving 7/10ths, with the top down, in reasonable comfort and considerable style, and don't mind having to deal with niggling maintenance/replacement issues on a fairly regular basis, the 1991–1993 Alfa Romeo Spider is a neat choice—particularly if it can be a second or third car that doesn't have to perform everyday duty. If you want a two-seat roadster that's more reliable and cheaper to run, consider a Miata. Just remember: it, or any other budget-priced 1990s-era sports car you're likely to look at will be missing that huge helping of Italian personality that makes the Spider such a special enthusiast machine.

SPECIFICATIONS (1992 SPIDER VELOCE)

Body style. . . . . Two door, two passenger
Drivetrain layout . . . . Front engine, rear drive
Engine type . . . . DOHC I-4
Displacement, liter/cc 2.0/1,962
Horsepower, hp @ rpm . . . . SAE net 120 @ 5,500
Torque, ft-lb @ rpm . . . . SAE net 117 @ 2,700
Transmission . . . . 5-speed manual
Wheelbase, in. 88.6
Length, in. 168.8 167.7
Width, in. 64.1 63.9
Height, in. 48.8 49.7
Base curb weight, lb. . . . . 2,750 (est) 2,550
Suspension, f/r . . . . Upper and lower A-arms/Live axle, Panhard rod
Steering type . . . . Worm and roller
Brakes, f/r . . . . Disc/disc

PERFORMANCE

Acceleration, 0–60 mph . . . . 10.8 sec.
Standing quarter
mile, sec/mph. 17.8/77
Source . . . . Road & Track

TYPICAL PARTS/REPAIR PRICES

Major tune-up/service. $610
Air filter 28
Shock absorber 80
Catalytic converter(s) 70
Clutch replacement 540

WEBSITE

alfaspider.com

REPORT CARD

Engine . . . . .A
Transmission . . . . .A
Power/Weight Ratio . . . .A-
Handling . . . . .A
Braking . . . . .A
Ride . . . . .B
Exterior Styling . . . . . . .A-
Interior Styling . . . . . . .B+
Interior Function . . . . . .A-
Cargo Capacity . . . . . . .B+
Everyday Usability C
Reliability . . . . .B-
Fit and Finish . . . . .A-
Market Availability . . . . .D
Resale Value Potential . . .A
Fun Factor . . . . .A+
Bang for Buck . . . . .A
Aftermarket Interest . . . .A
Club Support . . . . .A

BMW M3 (1990–1991)

Any BMW M model is automatically special. BMW's M sport entity is the heart of the company's performance and racing programs, and has lately become a "brand" of its own. Nowadays, BMW offers several different models that have benefited from the M treatment that blends well-balanced upgrades to performance, handling, and appearance. But it wasn't always so. There were sporadic appearances of M-tuned 5 and 6 Series cars through the 1980s, and the M treatment was given to the E30-bodied, U.S. market 3 Series for the first time in the 1987 model year. This limited-edition, high-performance two-door sport sedan continued in limited production until the introduction of the new, E36 chassis 3 Series for the 1992 model year.

What made these earliest M3s so special? Quite a bit, with all of it focused on the single-minded mission of impressive performance. The

Nobody will every accuse the E30 M3 as being anything but a thinly disguised race car. Subtlety is just not part of its deal. Most of the chrome went away in favor of a monochromatic paint job. *Klaus Schnitzer, courtesy BMW*

Bird's-eye view demonstrates the shape and width of the fenders' blister-style flares. This was required primarily for the racing version, which of course ran much wider rolling stock. *Klaus Schnitzer, courtesy BMW*

What makes an M an M? In this case, M stands for M Power and "motor"; the M3's hand-built 2.3-liter four put out nearly 200 horsepower, a lot for a naturally aspirated four—then and now. Note individual, race-inspired intake butterflies. *BMW*

M3 also served as a "homologation" special, meaning that a certain number needed to be built and sold to the public in order for the car to qualify for certain racing series. Another aspect of its near-cult status is rarity—just 1,148 cars were sold here during 1990–1991, with a total of less than 5,000 E30-bodied M3s sold from 1987 to 1991. Actually, the last of the cars were apparently tough to move, the final units not being sold until early 1993! You wouldn't know it now, as BMW enthusiasts and collectors hunt them down and pay dearly for good ones.

The center of the M3's appeal, as with most BMW M models, is its special engine. This race-bread unit is a high-winding, 2.3-liter, DOHC four, good for 192 horsepower at a lofty 6,750 rpm—redline was 500 rpm higher yet. This figure has only recently been equaled by other fours such as the VTEC unit found in the Honda Prelude—so it was certainly impressive in 1987. The engine features an intake system composed of individual throttle butterflies, and that impressive "BMW M Power" cam cover caps the cams. These engines are hand-built, and really beg for some enthusiastic driving. The only transmission offered was a five-speed manual.

Suspension upgrades included special front hubs, lower control arms, springs, shocks, suspension bushings, and anti-roll bars. The steering benefited from a quicker ratio, brakes were upgraded four-wheel discs, and the M3 rode on large-for-the-time 15x7-inch cast-alloy wheels. The emphasis, of course, was on handling, not ride quality. E30 M3s are athletic corner carvers to be sure, but offer up a street ride that's less than everyday friendly.

The bodywork got its share of attention as well, with special front and rear fascias, rocker panels, deck spoiler, and a revised trunk and rear window treatment that had better aerodynamics than the standard 3 Series. Remember—this model was brought to market largely to satisfy racing organizations by proving that it was, indeed, a production model. All four fenders were flared, and the look was that of a—well—race car for the street. The interior also benefited from thickly bolstered sport seats and a special steering wheel.

If you enjoy a visceral machine, these early M3s are quite a ride. The engine thrums and vibrates a bit, the reflexes are quick, the brakes firm, and the cornering limits relatively high. It doesn't feel very impressive at lower rpms, but once past about 4,500, the M

The M3 evidences a lot of aerodynamic changes at the rear end, which includes flat, raised rear wing and higher deck lid. None of it makes much difference at street speed—but it sure looks cool. *Klaus Schnitzer, courtesy BMW*

motor really wakes up and offers an impressive pull up to about 7,000. But many of the important luxury touches were either standard or optional, such as leather interior, air conditioning, sunroof, and power windows and locks. The only substantive hardware change during its five-model-year run was the addition of a driver-side air bag in 1990.

M3s are not that expensive to buy, but they can be very expensive to own. These engines love their oil changes, hopefully not at more than 3,000-mile intervals. A number of service items need to be addressed every 7,500 miles, and a valve adjustment—something foreign to many car owners expecting 100,000-mile tune-up intervals—every 15,000 miles. Accessory engine mounts (those for things like the alternator and power steering pump) tend to crack.

There are quite a few bushings in the chassis subframe that age and wear out, causing sloppy handling and a degradation in ride quality. Exhaust gaskets tend to blow out, causing exhaust leaks and noise. In short, the M3 is one of the most extreme examples of where paying a premium price for a low-mileage, meticulously maintained car ends up being a bargain, over an abused, worn-out—no matter how low its purchase price may seem. Verifying an M3's service record is critical. If cared for, the engine is tough and well built, as is the transmission. Clutches should be good for

75,000 miles, more if the driver has been a smooth shifter. The rear differential will probably need some service at around 100,000 miles or so. Everything else holds up pretty well, in keeping with BMW's reputation for high-quality materials and solid construction.

Also know that these are popular club racers, and many have seen some track time. This by itself is not a reason to stay away, but the stresses of maximum revs, cornering limits, and braking do wear out a car faster. Fortunately, virtually every part necessary to maintain an M3—both standard BMW items and M3 specific hardware—is available, both from the factory or the aftermarket. But none of it comes cheap.

Perhaps offsetting some of the above is the fact that M3s have likely depreciated as far as they're going to (remember, less than 5,000 sold over five model years). So while it may be hard to classify them as investments, they are likely to hold value from now on, and perhaps even increase as time goes on.

As you've probably guessed, these early M3s are not for the casual enthusiast. They need lots of care and feeding, and a bad one can be a money pit. They're special, quite rare, and a thrill to drive but a little edgy for use as an everyday commuter. But if you find a good one, and maintain it properly, you'll have a real driving machine that's also likely to hold its value better than most of the cars in this book.

SPECIFICATIONS (1990 M3)

Body style . . . . Two door, five passenger
Drivetrain layout. . . . . Front engine, front drive
Engine type . . . . DOHC I-4
Displacement, liter/cc 2.3/2,302
Horsepower, hp @ rpm . . . . SAE net 192 @ 6,750
Torque, ft-lb @ rpm . . . . SAE net 170 @ 4,750
Transmission . . . . 5-speed manual
Wheelbase, in. 101.0
Length, in. 171.1
Width, in.. . . . . 66.1
Height, in. 53.9
Base curb weight, lb 2,865
Suspension, f/r. . . . . MacPherson strut/semi-trailing arm
Steering type . . . . Recalculating ball
Brakes, f/r. . . . . Disc/disc

PERFORMANCE

Acceleration, 0–60 mph . . . . 7.1 sec.
Standing quarter
mile, sec/mph 15.4/91.0
Source. . . . . Road & Track

TYPICAL PARTS/REPAIR PRICES

Major tune-up/service. $850
Air filter 13
Shock absorber 52
Catalytic converter(s) 81
Clutch replacement. 1,028

WEBSITE

artglenn.com/bmwm3

REPORT CARD

Engine	A
Transmission	A
Power/Weight Ratio	B
Handling	A-
Braking	A-
Ride	A-
Exterior Styling	A-
Interior Styling	A-
Interior Function	A
Cargo Capacity	A-
Everyday Usability	A
Reliability	A-
Fit and Finish	A
Market Availability	A-
Resale Value Potential	B
Fun Factor	B
Bang for Buck	B
Aftermarket Interest	A
Club Support	A

BMW 3 Series Coupe (1993–1999)

Some will argue that a BMW 3 Series represents a certain zenith among sport sedans. So why do we include them in a discussion of sports and GT cars? Simple: they're awfully sporty, in some cases more so than many supposed sports cars. And they are exceptionally satisfying to drive. Add to that BMW's reputation as a premium brand, and the 3's considerable motorsports history.

BMW gave the 3 Series a complete remodel for 1992, launching the new E36-platform cars in sedan form only. The two-door came along for 1993, and a convertible followed along for the 1994 model year. Both four- (318) and six-cylinder (325)-powered models were offered, though we'll restrict our discussion to only the latter. Why? The four-cylinder 3's just aren't that quick (though they certainly handle well). In the used car market, the six-cylinder cars cost slightly more, and offer the power to

BMW launched its E36-bodied 3 Series in 1992, but the coupe model waited a year before breaking cover. The two-door is more of a different car than you might think, and shares very few body panels. This is a 1993 325is. *BMW*

Many enthusiasts want a convertible but can't get by with a small two-seater sports car either; this 325i makes a great choice, though its chassis is not quite as stiff structurally as the coupe's, and therefore doesn't handle with quite the same precision when pushed really hard. Still, a nice balance between performance and sunshine. *BMW*

make the most of the 3 Series' well-developed chassis. Same goes for the four-cylinder only, 318ti hatchback, which was really more of a VW Golf competitor.

The 1993 325is coupe was not an inexpensive car (few BMWs are) but packed serious hardware: a torsionally stiff rear-wheel drive chassis, fully independent suspension, four-wheel disc brakes (vented up front) with standard ABS, speed-sensitive power rack-and-pinion steering, a driver-side air bag, power windows/seats/locks, an AM/FM/cassette stereo, leather-trimmed seats and steering wheel, the choice of a five-speed manual or four-speed automatic transmission, and a 2.5-liter, DOHC inline six rated at 189 horsepower. Few V-6s deliver the same smooth, satisfying whir of power as does an inline six, particularly one from BMW. Straight sixes have been one of BMW's best-known calling cards for decades, and remain so today. The optional automatic offers three shift modes: Manual, Economy, and Sport; a limited-slip differential is also optional.

As noted, a stylish convertible was introduced for 1994. Unlike some converts, the E36 3 Series body/chassis was designed with a convertible in mind from the beginning. So it's not an afterthought "chop job"; all requisite chassis reinforcements were engineered in. The power top is fully lined and nicely padded. The rear window is glass, and a rear defroster is also included. The convert weighs a few hundred pounds more than the coupe, though the reduction in performance is minimal.

The 3 Series interior is well finished and businesslike. Particularly satisfying is the 3's "cockpit-style" dash arrangement, which orients the gauges and controls toward the driver—a style that's been copied by many others. And it's hard to fault BMW's build and engineering quality either: everything fits, clicks, and snaps with a feeling of precision.

That comes across in the driving experience too; there's plenty of power from an engine that loves to rev. Braking power is more than adequate, and road feel

29

This is the budget-priced—for a BMW anyway—323i convertible. The real performance enthusiast won't prefer this model, as it combines the heavier convertible body style (due mostly to the hardware required to operate the top, and the extra chassis stiffening) with the smaller engine. So it's a bit more of a cruiser than a racer. But it's an awfully nice cruiser, and you still benefit from BMW's outstanding chassis tuning and rear-wheel drive. *BMW*

through the steering wheel is exceptional too. The nicely contoured seats grip you firmly, all controls fall at hand, and the 325is proves to be a willing handler in a way that only a German, rear-wheel drive car can be. While some others may ultimately provide higher cornering grip, there are few cars that communicate with the driver as well as a BMW, and these E36 cars are no exception. The sedan-like profile means lots of glass, good visibility, a reasonable trunk, and adequate room in back for kids or smallish adults in a pinch.

1994 was largely a carryover year, with the exception of the introduction of the convertible body style. A passenger-side air bag was added as standard equipment, a new traction control system was offered as an option, and the automatic's gear ratios were shuffled for slightly crisper acceleration. 1995 again saw relatively few changes, such as the addition of a new Premium Package option, which included a height-adjustable steering wheel, a trip computer, and wood trim.

The 3 Series mid-life update arrived in 1996, and it was a good one. Displacement increased from 2.5 to 2.8 liters, and while the horsepower rating only increased by 1 (from 189 to 190), the goal, and the real improvement, came in terms of increased torque. The 328is' larger six is rated at 207 ft-lb of torque, an increase of 14 percent over the 2.5's 181-pound-foot rating. Its low-end torque moved the car away from the light or out of a corner, and the newfound power helped turn a great car into an even better one. There were other numerous mechanical improvements to the engine and exhaust system, and EPA-rated fuel mileage even increased. Other changes included a new standard automatic climate control system and upgraded sound systems, plus the availability of a Sports Package option for the convertible. In addition, 0–60 time dropped to around 7.0 seconds for a 328is five-speed.

1997 brought a subtle restyling in the form of slightly reshaped front grilles, new marker lights and turn signals, a body-colored trunk grip, a redesigned interior console, and heated outside mirrors. The top on the convertible model was also updated for fully automatic operation: no more latches with which to mess, just press the button, and the top locks and unlocks itself.

By 1998, everyone knew that a new 3 Series would be on its way soon, but BMW still invested the effort to update the current model. The big change was the introduction of a new 323 model, available in coupe, convertible, and sedan form. In spite of the "23" moniker, which one would think indicates a 2.3-liter engine, the new-for-1998 323is was in fact powered by a 2.5-liter six, so in effect, it represented the reintroduction of the previous 325 model. The major difference is a slightly lower state of tune: 168 horsepower versus the previous 325's 189 horse rating.

However, the price was thousands of dollars less than the 328, so it represented a good balance between performance and cost.

An all-new 3 Series did in fact come along for 1999, though it was introduced in sedan form only, so the previous 328 and 323 models carried over for most of that year, until production ran out.

One option worth mentioning is the Sports Package. It was available on most 3 Series models, and includes firmer suspension calibrations, larger wheels and tires, power sport seats, and the trip computer. It adds an additional measure of edge to the 325/328is. Although the lack of this option shouldn't keep you from buying a well-cared-for, low-mileage, right-priced 3 Series, it's worth finding a car that has it if possible. It shouldn't add more than $500–1,000 to the price of the car, and is a bargain at that.

Even though the new-for-1998 323is's badge would have you think it carries a 2.3-liter engine, it's really a 2.5 (don't ask; we don't understand it either). Although it wasn't as highly tuned as that of the original 325, the 323 still represented an excellent, cost-effective way to get into a six-cylinder 3 Series. *BMW*

BMW's are well-engineered, stoutly built cars that are good for really long miles—if given exceptional care. The six-cylinder engines are just about bulletproof, and if given fresh spark plugs every 30,000 miles, a fresh oil and filter every 3,000–5,000, and hose/belt changes as required, should be good for 150,000 miles without the need for major service. Manual transmissions are equally good, but will need attention by 100K. The automatic is a fully sealed unit, requiring no oil or filter services of its own; it too should go at least 100,000 miles before overhaul is required.

According to an Owner's Survey article in *Road & Track,* the most common problem centered on faulty windshield wipers. BMWs tend to be somewhat hard on tires, perhaps due to the fact that they inspire spirited driving. Brake rotors are made of a somewhat soft metal, which makes for excellent, squeak-free performance, but they tend to wear out quickly because of it. Some of the engine management system sensors tend to be troublesome, requiring more-frequent-than-average replacement.

Exhaust systems are usually shot by 100,000 miles and are expensive to replace. In fact, this last comment tends to reflect the situation for most BMW service components: long lasting but expensive to replace. Labor rates are on the higher side, somewhat expected with a premium brand. Interior materials are of generally higher quality than found on some Japanese and American brands, though a sun-cracked dash is not uncommon, and again, expensive to replace.

If a sporty, communicative driving experience is important to you, the BMW 325/328/323is is among the more impressive cars in this book. There are others that are cheaper, and some that have more out and out horsepower, but the 3 Series combines sublime driving characteristics in an everyday-usable, high-quality, name-brand package that tends to last long and hold its value.

(Below and opposite) Nothing moves the car better than torque, and the new for 1996 328is delivered increased torque and horsepower as compared to the early 325s. Exterior changes are minor but kept the car looking fresh. *BMW*

BMW cockpits have always been considered "driver oriented," and this photo shows why. The controls are canted toward the driver, the gauges are clear and crisply marked, and the steering wheel is thickly padded and feels good to the hand. Many actually prefer the ease of operation of this nonautomatic HVAC system, with its large twist controls, to that of many cars that require the driver to scroll through digital operations just to get some air. *Rik Paul photo, courtesy* Motor Trend

In what seems to be a world of V-6 engines, BMW has stuck with inline sixes and is probably better for it. The smoothness, sound, and torque of a BMW straight six are what put the company on the map in the United States in the 1960s. This is the later 2.8-liter unit. *BMW*

SPECIFICATIONS (1993 325is)

Body style . . . . Two door, five passenger
Drivetrain layout . . . . Front engine, rear drive
Engine type . . . . DOHC I-6
Displacement, liter/cc 2.5/2,494
Horsepower, hp @ rpm . . . . SAE net 189 @ 5,900
Torque, ft-lb @ rpm . . . . SAE net 181 @ 4,700
Transmission . . . . 5-speed manual
Wheelbase, in. 106.3
Length, in. 174.5
Width, in. 67.3
Height, in. 53.8
Base curb weight, lb 3,065
Suspension, f/r . . . . MacPherson strut/multilink
Steering type. . . . . Rack and pinion
Brakes, f/r. . . . . Disc/disc

PERFORMANCE

Acceleration, 0–60 mph . . . . 8.3 sec.
Standing quarter
mile, sec/mph 16.2/87.0
Source. . . . . Road & Track

TYPICAL PARTS/REPAIR PRICES

Major tune-up/service. $850
Air filter 13
Shock absorber 52
Catalytic converter(s) 81
Clutch replacement 1,028

WEBSITES

bmwcca.com
bmwna.com

Chapter 6

FOR
- Big, American-style V-8 power
- Swoopy styling
- Performance/value ratio

AGAINST
- Fit and finish not up to Euro/Asian standards
- Back seat really cramped
- Loves gas

HOT PICK
1998 Z28

REPORT CARD

Engine . . . . .A
Transmission . . . . .A
Power/Weight Ratio . . . .A
Handling . . . . .B-
Braking . . . . .B-
Ride . . . . .B-
Exterior Styling . . . . . . .A
Interior Styling . . . . . . .C+
Interior Function . . . . . .C-
Cargo Capacity . . . . . . .C-
Everyday Usability . . . . .B
Reliability . . . . .B
Fit and Finish C
Market Availability . . . .A-
Resale Value Potential . . .B-
Fun Factor . . . . .A-
Bang for Buck . . . . .A-
Aftermarket Interest . . . .A-
Club Support . . . . .B

Chevrolet Camaro Z28 (1993–1999)

Ford was caught totally by surprise when GM rolled out its new-for-1993 "F Body" coupes, the redesigned Chevrolet Camaro and Pontiac Firebird. Ford had planned on using carryover drivetrains from its previous-generation Mustang when it rolled out a new one for 1994. That meant trusty 5.0 V-8s to be rated at 215 horsepower. But when GM pulled the trigger on the new F cars, the bullets fired were 275 horsepower versions of the Corvette's LT1 5.7-liter V-8. Ford has been playing horsepower catch-up ever since.

That's only one reason to consider buying one. The other is that, at least for the time being, the current-generation Camaro (and Firebird) is the last of its breed, that is, rear-drive, V-8-powered muscle coupe. 2002 could be this model's last year, with no replacement in the works. We

The Camaro was an all-new car for 1993, and really raised the bar in terms of musclecar performance and handling. Up until then, the Mustang regularly waxed the Camaro in all the magazine performance tests, but no longer: its 275-horse small-block V-8 gave it an advantage that Ford has yet to really catch up with. *Chevrolet*

Chevy spent big bucks to launch the new Camaro, as it served twice as the Indy 500 Pace Car during the 1990s: a 1993 model is seen at the upper right, with a 1997 Pace Car Edition Z28 in the foreground. The other cars, from left, are a 1967, 1969, and 1982. *Chevrolet*

suspect it won't be the end of the Camaro as a nameplate, but it may come back in very different—and perhaps not as exciting—form.

GM's goal was to meld an exotic body shape with American-style power, and some brakes and handling to match. On balance, it was successful in doing so. As noted, the Z28's V-8 was rated at 275 horsepower, backed by either a four-speed automatic overdrive transmission or the much-desired Borg Warner T-56 six-speed manual. Although the V-6 powered RS is nothing to sneeze at (especially in 1997-and-later, 3.8-liter 200-horsepower form), the Z28 is really the performance bargain here, and thus the model we recommend.

The Z was offered in essentially two body styles: a 2+2 coupe and a convertible. Some might consider the T-top model as a third, but it's really just an option for the closed coupe. A wide variety of options were available,

from sound systems and power accessories, to leather upholstery and the Z51 performance suspension. But the heart of the Camaro is the aforementioned LT1 V-8. Its prodigious horsepower and torque output nearly rival that of the 'Vette's; it is indeed the same powerplant, only slightly de-tuned via slightly more restrictive intake and exhaust systems (the Corvette powerplant, as introduced in 1992, was rated at 300 horses). It's great fun to take through the gears, and makes those wonderful V-8 noises.

Camaro's development was gradual from 1993 through 1996. A power output rating increase (to 285 horsepower) came along in 1996. 1997 represented the first of a two-year remodeling program the Camaro (and Firebird) were about to undertake. The powertrain and bodywork carried over; most of the changes were found inside. Not everyone was pleased with the Camaro's interior when it was introduced in

1993: there were odd-looking "blister"-shaped cooling vents atop the dash, and all of the allen-head screws were fake plastic pieces. The typefaces on the gauges mocked those of a digital readout, and the radio was mounted low on the console, comfortably obscured by the shifter. The whole thing looked a bit plasticky and immature.

Things got better for 1997 with a much-improved cabin. The dash layout was cleaned up for a more upscale appearance; it was also constructed of fewer pieces of plastic, in the hopes of fewer squeaks and rattles. Instruments were revised for better looks and readability. Soft-to-the-touch materials replaced hard plastics, and the radio and HVAC controls switched spots. Upgraded sound systems included a trunk-mounted CD player for the first time. The only negative is that the seats were redesigned for greater comfort; but those "improvements" came at the cost of some of the seats' side bolstering, making them less grippy during aggressive cornering maneuvers. Other than that, the new interior is a much nicer place.

Exterior changes were few; new five-spoke wheel designs replaced the previous "blender-blade" alloy, and the taillight clusters now sported amber turn signals. Daytime running lights became standard. An interesting special option for the 1997 was the optional 30th Anniversary Appearance Package that reaches right back to 1967 for inspiration. The 30th Anniversary Z was finished in white with Hugger Orange striping, and the seats were covered in an oh-so-1960s houndstooth fabric. You could find 30th Anniversary emblems everywhere. It's rare that any of these "anniversary editions" really look good or become exceptionally collectible; the 30th Anniversary Camaro is no exception, unless you are particularly nostalgic. Buy one if you like it, but don't pay much extra for it. Overall, the 1997 Camaro is a bit of a one-year model, as it combined the 1993–1996 exterior appearance, along with the 1998 and later interior. Those that prefer the early look would do well to seek out a 1997.

The Camaro's exterior was virtually unchanged from 1993 through 1997; this 1997 incorporates a new five-spoke wheel design and amber-colored rear turn signal lamps (neither of which is too obvious in this picture, but that's one reason an early Z is almost as desirable as a later one). *Chevrolet*

One of the Camaro Z28's most interesting design aspects is the way the rear fenders and rear deck create a rear deck spoiler without it looking like a tacked-on piece. This is a 1994 Z28 coupe. *Chevrolet*

Camaro's remodel continued for 1998, and the improvements plucked the heartstrings of the muscle-car faithful. Out went the previous Corvette-based LT1 285-horse V-8, and in went a slightly de-tuned version of the new-for-1997 Corvette's LS1 V-8, good for 305 horses. Even though the displacement remained 5.7 liters, and an overhead valve arrangement was retained, this was an all-new powerplant. Now, both heads and block are cast alloy, and the LS1 employed advancements such as a distributorless ignition. The new V-8 is lighter, more powerful, more fuel efficient, smoother, and burns cleaner than the engine it replaced.

Along with the new engine came a new front-end treatment, with glinty, glassed-in headlights and a somewhat rectangular-shaped grille area. There was also a much-upgraded brake system (larger discs, revised ABS) for surer pedal feel and more consistent stops, and a newer -generation traction control system—thankfully still including an on/off switch for those who love their burnouts. Camaro finished out the decade with no additional changes; the 1999s were carryover duplicates of the 1998 models.

By now, you're probably asking about the even higher performance Camaro SS models. SS—Chevy-speak for Super Sport—was a popular Camaro option/model during the 1960s and early 1970s, and reappeared for 1996. Those first modern-era SSs were actually converted from standard Z28s by a company in Michigan named Street Legal Performance (SLP). A revised air cleaner system, cold air intake hood, and free-flow exhaust system conspired to increase horsepower from 285 to 305 horsepower. Other changes included 17-inch five-spoke alloy wheels and SS identification. Even though an outside shop did the work, the SS is considered a factory piece, as it could be ordered and delivered through any Chevy dealer and was fully warranted. The LS1-powered SS increased the horsepower ante from the now-standard 305 to a nearly 'Vette-like 320.

There's no question that these are the ultimate performance Camaros of the 1990s, though they are still likely to be well outside our $20K ceiling as of this writing. Most of the SS components were available on an aftermarket basis, so make sure you are buying a

Drop the top, and burn rubber: this photo shows the first Camaro 1994 Z28 convertible coming down the production line. Although the Camaro is definitely an American car in spirit, it's actually produced in Canada. Since the car was originally designed with a convertible version in mind, there is reasonably little loss in the way of structural integrity, though there is definitely some small amount of cowl shake present on really rough surfaces. *Chevrolet*

real SS before paying a premium over that of a standard Z28.

From a driving standpoint, the Z28 is as American as the proverbial apple pie. Acceleration is its No. 1 calling card. While handling and braking are not nearly as sharp as, say, a BMW M3, they do offer adequate steady state cornering, good grip, and, of course, can practically be steered with the throttle. They're certainly not the most practical cars ever built: visibility is marginal, the rear seats are almost useless save for pets and grocery bags, and trunk space is also limited.

Mechanically, GM F-bodies are quite sturdy. Given reasonable care and minimal abuse, the engines will go 125,000–150,000 miles before needing major overhaul. Both automatic and manual transmissions

are tough as well, though throw-out bearings usually begin making noise at 60,000–70,000 miles on the six-speed cars. And make sure that the six-speed manual is in good shape: it's an expensive tranny to replace or repair. Exhaust systems tend to leak, though that's an easy muffler shop fix.

Fit and finish quality don't generally measure up to the best European makes, so things like interior panels wear easily (though the standard seat cloth holds up well). We've seen too many five-year-old Camaros with faded paint, indicating they require constant care and waxing to keep up. The 1993–1996 cars tend to have more squeaks and rattles than later Camaros. And if 0–60 is your favorite statistic, you won't find a cheaper way to get there than a 1993–1999 Camaro Z28.

Under $20K? Not likely: this limited-edition 30th Anniversary convertible will likely hold its value for some time to come. It replicates the white, orange, and houndstooth interior treatment offered on the first 1967s. *Chevrolet*

Part of why people often call the Z28 the "son of Corvette" is that it actually shares its basic engine with Chevy's top-line two seater. This LT1 V-8 of 1993 put out 285 horsepower as opposed to the Corvette's rating of 300 for the same year—Chevrolet always makes sure that the 'Vette remains the king of its performance hill. But only by a little. *Chevrolet*

Front-end restyling for 1998 would carry the car through the rest of the decade. Although this car happens to be a 2000 model, the front-end treatment is the same as the 1998/1999, including glassed-in headlamps and reconfigured front fascia. The scoop indicates this Camaro is an SS model, and the car in the background is the photographer's own 1967 SS convertible. *John Kiewicz, Motor Trend*

The interior update that came along for 1997 was a huge improvement: fewer plastic pieces means fewer rough edges, and the potential for fewer rattles. Faux-digital dash graphics gave way to a cleaner look, and the strange "blister" vent design was also redone. This is the retro-inspired, if not exactly subtle, houndstooth-check interior trim found on the 1997 30th Anniversary Camaro, though the dash design carried through to all models.

SPECIFICATIONS (1996 CAMARO Z28)

Body style. . . . . Two door, four passenger
Drivetrain layout . . . . Front engine, rear drive
Engine type . . . . OHV V-8
Displacement, liter/cc 5.7/5,737
Horsepower, hp @ rpm . . . . SAE net 285 @ 5,200
Torque, ft-lb @ rpm . . . . SAE net 325 @ 2,400
Transmission . . . . 6-speed manual
Wheelbase, in. 101.1
Length, in. 193.2
Width, in. 74.1
Height, in. 51.3
Base curb weight, lb 3,442
Suspension, f/r . . . . Upper and lower A-arms/live axle
Steering type. . . . . Rack and pinion
Brakes, f/r. . . . . Disc/disc

PERFORMANCE

Acceleration, 0–60 mph . . . . 5.9 sec.
Standing quarter
mile, sec/mph 14.5/96.6
Source . . . . Road & Track

TYPICAL PARTS/REPAIR PRICES

Major tune-up/service. $700
Air filter 10
Shock absorber 81
Catalytic converter(s) 108
Clutch replacement 1,200

WEBSITES

camaroclub.com
camaro.com

Chapter 7

FOR
- Fabulous LT1 engine
- High handling ability
- Removable roof panel or convertible

AGAINST
- Fiberglass body creaks
- High insurance rates
- Tacky interior

HOT PICK
1996 Corvette Coupe

REPORT CARD

Engine	A
Transmission	A
Power/Weight Ratio	A
Handling	B+
Braking	B+
Ride	B-
Exterior Styling	A-
Interior Styling	C
Interior Function	C+
Cargo Capacity	C
Everyday Usability	B-
Reliability	B
Fit and Finish	C
Market Availability	B+
Resale Value Potential	B
Fun Factor	A-
Bang for Buck	A
Aftermarket Interest	A
Club Support	A

Chevrolet Corvette (1992–1996)

Until the appearance of Dodge's Viper, the Chevrolet Corvette was legitimately labeled "American's Only True Sports Car." And it's true. The 'Vette has always been true to its roots: a fiberglass-bodied, two-seat sports car powered by an overhead valve V-8 (if you discount the 1953–1954 models, which used six-cylinder engines, and the much later ZR1s, which employed overhead cams). In between the current and pricey "C5" Corvettes and those collectible classics of the 1950s and 1960s lie the last of the "C4"-generation 'Vettes that represent a good balance between performance and price.

The C4 cars, so named as they represented the fourth platform on which the Corvette was based since its 1953 debut, were built from 1984 through 1996. Those earliest C4s were plagued with problems and poorly chosen components, but the car was steadily improved throughout the balance of the 1980s and into the early 1990s. Why focus on the

This photo demonstrates two of the three C4 Corvette body styles offered during the 1990s. The third? The slightly-wider-at-the-rear ZR1, which is well out of this book's price ceiling. *David Newhardt*

1992 and later 'Vettes? First and foremost because they enjoyed a new-for-1992 powerplant upgrade, called the LT1 V-8.

Good for an impressive 300 horsepower, the LT1 engine represented a substantive redo of the good old small-block Chevy. It benefited from reverse-flow cooling, a more modern engine management system, a crankshaft-driven water pump and distributor system—and, of course, the owner benefited from an impressive 50 horsepower increase over the 1990–1991 cars. There's nothing wrong with a 1990 or 1991 Corvette, but the 1992-and-later cars are much better performers for not a lot more money.

These late C4 'Vettes were offered in two body styles: fastback coupe, which features a removable center roof section, or as a full convertible. Either can be had with a ZF six-speed manual transmission or a GM four-speed automatic. The days of buying a lightweight Corvette especially equipped for drag racing (no radio, heater, power steering, or power brakes to save weight) had disappeared long ago; the Corvette was a reasonably equipped car. Standard hardware

Yes—this is a pre-1992 Corvette, but it illustrates one of the car's most vulnerable areas, that being the lower front fascia. Although it is made of a pliable hard plastic material, it's easily damaged by high curbs and other road obstacles. *David Newhardt*

included power four-wheel disc brakes with ABS; power steering, windows, and locks; air conditioning; cruise control; an anti-theft system; a limited-slip differential; an electronic traction control system (which, thankfully, can be switched off should the driver wish to summon some oversteer with his right foot); and a stainless-steel exhaust. GM is notorious for under-equipping its cars in the wheel and tire department, but doesn't short shrift the Corvette; it got standard 17-inch alloys and high-performance Goodyear Eagle GS radials.

Corvettes have always been, to a certain extent, about image, but the LT1-powered cars really did live up to the look. The 0–60 times were usually in the 5.5–6.0-second range, depending on the magazine doing the testing, and whether the car was a stick or automatic. The automatic is a decent enough piece, very robust, and with ratios that suited the engine's wide power band. But it's not in any way high tech; don't look for sequential shift technology, multiple modes, or even a fifth ratio. The real sports car enthusiast will be much happier with the six-speed, which is also a very tough unit and a joy to drive.

You'll notice we haven't mentioned the rare-ish ZR-1 'Vettes built from 1990 to 1995. These cars

boasted a 3-inch wider rear track and bodywork than a standard model, and were powered by a double-overhead cammed-, four-valve-per-cylinder V-8 built for Chevrolet by Mercury Marine. Why? 'Vette collectors seek these cars out, prices are nowhere near our $20K limit, and are not likely to be for some time.

The Corvette had received a facelift for 1991, and nose, tail, and wheel-design revisions would carry the car from the first LT1 model of 1992 through the C4's final model year, 1996. Models for 1993 were virtually unchanged, though 1994 brought a revised, electronically controlled automatic transmission and a standard, passenger-side air bag. 1995 was again a carry-over year, and 1996 saw the introduction of two, one-year only commemorative models: the Sebring Silver Collector Edition, and the Grand Sport, which included an LT4 version of the base powerplant that put out an even more impressive 330 horsepower. The LT4 was optional on all 1996 Corvettes, though standard on the Grand Sport. Don't expect to find either of these "last-of-the-C4" special editions for less than $20K for a long time.

Not everyone is a fan of the C4's interior, as its plastics, materials, and fit and finish aren't up to the quality standards of most Japanese compacts. But it's a

Things really got interesting for the C4 Corvette when it received all-new LT1 powertrains for 1992. This 1992 convertible represents a good buy among C4s, as power output, and most equipment levels, hardly changed for the next five years. *Chevrolet*

Chevy was again the Pace Car for the Indy 500, this time with a special 1995 LT1 Corvette. The car is based on a convertible model, with a special and safety bar at the back for pace car duty. Naturally, a street version of the pace car was offered, though the look of its graphics and paint treatment is a little wild for the street. *Chevrolet*

By the time the LT1-powered, final-generation C4 Corvettes came along, the cabins were much improved over the earlier, mid-1980s models. The instrumentation had been redesigned to employ mostly analog gauges, though a few ancillary functions still relied on digital readouts. Still, it's all a bit plasticky. The slick, six-speed shifter is a joy to use. *Chevrolet*

close-coupled cockpit, you sit low to the ground, and it certainly feels sporty. Leather upholstery was optional, though it found its way onto a very high percentage of these cars. Be prepared to live with more-than-the-usual number of squeaks and rattles due to the fiberglass bodywork and separate frame arrangement—it's just part of the experience of owning any Corvette.

There are a few problem areas but few real secrets about these cars, because their extremely loyal ownership base, club network, and strong aftermarket have figured out a fix, or an upgrade, for their every foible. Given reasonable care, oil changes, and a minimum of abuse, the drivetrain is exceptionally tough and long-lived. LT1 engines should go 150,000 miles without needing anything except tune-ups and fluid changes. Both transmissions are equally stout, except the clutches on manual cars start getting noisy at around 75,000 miles, and will absolutely need replacement by 100,000.

Alternators tend to go our fairly often, but are not expensive to replace. Steering racks tend to get rough or noisy as early as 60,000 miles, and unfortunately that is not a cheap fix, so make sure the one on the car you're looking at is in good shape, or negotiate accordingly. Finally, Corvettes tend to wear out tires for several reasons, only one of which may be aggressive driving. The other is that they require both front- and rear-end wheel alignments, and owners tend to skip or forget the one in back. Unless the owner has a receipt for a recent, complete alignment, this would be something to take care of immediately upon purchase. All the suspension bushings will need replacement by 100,000 miles.

If the "loud 'n' proud," all-American Corvette appeals to you, you'll love its acceleration and capable handling capabilities. Its style still turns heads and garners good parking places from valets. Be prepared to live with marginal gas mileage, the aforementioned squeaky nature, and a minimum of cargo space. Given care, they also tend to hold their values reasonably well, are quite reliable, and of course, a ball to drive.

SPECIFICATIONS (1992 CORVETTE)

Body style . . . . Two door, two passenger
Drivetrain layout . . . . Front engine, rear drive
Engine type . . . . OHV V-8
Displacement, liter/cc 5.7/5,733
Horsepower, hp @ rpm . . . . SAE net 300 @ 5,000
Torque, ft-lb @ rpm . . . . SAE net 330 @ 4,000
Transmission . . . . 6-speed manual
Wheelbase, in. 96.2
Length, in. 178.6
Width, in. 71.0
Height, in. 46.7
Base curb weight, lb 3,330
Suspension, f/r . . . . Upper and lower A-arms/multi-link
Steering type. . . . . Rack and pinion
Brakes, f/r . . . . Disc/disc

PERFORMANCE

Acceleration, 0–60 mph, ... 5.7 sec.
Standing quarter
mile, sec/mph 14.1/102.00
Source . . . . Motor Trend

TYPICAL PARTS/REPAIR PRICES

Major tune-up/service. $280
Air filter 23
Shock absorber 81
Catalytic converter(s) 154
Clutch replacement 800

WEBSITE

corvetteclubofamerica.com

REPORT CARD

Engine	B
Transmission	B
Power/Weight Ratio	B+
Handling	B
Braking	B
Ride	B
Exterior Styling	B
Interior Styling	B
Interior Function	B
Cargo Capacity	B
Everyday Usability	A-
Reliability	B
Fit and Finish	B
Market Availability	B-
Resale Value Potential	C+
Fun Factor	B+
Bang for Buck	A-
Aftermarket Interest	B-
Club Support	B

Dodge Neon R/T (1998–1999)

You need only look at the Dodge Neon R/T's "skunk stripes," gunsight grille, and rounded front fog lights to know that its goal in life is to be a pint-sized Viper for people of more moderate incomes. While nobody could actually confuse a 150-horsepower R/T with the 450-horsepower RT/10, it does come from the same family, and packs a reasonable performance punch of its own—especially for the price.

The Neon R/T (for "Road/Track," a long-time Dodge performance label) was only on the market for two model years. No Plymouth-branded version was ever offered.

The R/T was developed out of the ACR, or "American Club Racing," model. When the Neon was first introduced in 1994 as a 1995 model, Dodge felt it was an ideal candidate for SCCA Showroom Stock racing. The ACR was a low-volume, lightweight Neon that did away with weight-adding extras, and offered additional performance-related options, such as a stiff suspension and lower gear ratios. While street

The R/T package's Viper-flavored styling cues make the most of the Neon's shape. Still, it's a shame that Dodge didn't have just a few more pennies in the budget to give the R/T larger, more aggressive wheels and tires, as it would fortify the R/T's look, and probably boost its handling ability. Fortunately, since these cars are so inexpensive, there should be a few bucks left over for some aftermarket upgrades. *DaimlerChrysler*

Many lamented the passing of the Nissan Sentra SE-R, and felt that its personality lived on in the Neon R/T. We agree, though it certainly should have been given 15-inch wheels to further improve handling and beef up its appearance. *DaimlerChrysler*

legal, only the most die-hard Neon fan would want one as a daily driver—the earliest ACR's were not even available with air conditioning, and none have ever offered ABS, power windows, leather interior, etc. Dodge took most of the ACR's performance hardware, mixed in the Viper-inspired trim, made the more popular optional equipment available, and created the R/T.

Only one drivetrain was offered, that being the Neon's top-of-the-line DOHC 16-valve four serving up 150 horsepower and 133 ft-lb of torque. R/Ts were only offered with a five-speed manual transmission. Besides the aforementioned stripes and fog lights, all R/Ts had 14-inch alloy wheels, a rear deck spoiler, and "power bulge" hood to distinguish them from garden-variety Neons. Inside, full instrumentation included an 8,000-rpm tach (actual redline is a heady 7,200), sport bucket seats, and a leather-wrapped steering wheel and shift knob.

R/T suspension tuning was more aggressive than the standard Neon and Neon Sport, but not as much as the ACR. Springs were stiffer, there were sway bars front and rear, and the R/T also got a quicker steering gear and four-wheel disc brakes—often not available on cars costing a lot more. Most came with popular options such as AC, power windows, and anti-lock brakes, and color selection was limited to white, blue, black, and red. R/T was a bargain, starting out in 1998

at less than $14,000, with fully loaded examples running around $16K.

The earliest Neons were plagued by quality control problems and excessive noise, vibration, and harshness (NVH). Materials quality on those early cars wasn't exactly up to the standards set by many of its German and Japanese competitors either. But by the time the R/T showed up in 1998, most of those issues had been addressed: the Neon had become a pleasant, well-built car that generally offered more performance than other compacts costing the same amount of money. The engine is still not Honda-smooth but enjoys being flogged to 7,000 rpm. The ACR-bred suspension gives it really worthwhile handling, and the brakes, as you'd expect, are exceptional. The interior is handsome, comfortable, and reasonably well appointed, though the coupe's thick C-pillar creates a bit of a blind spot.

The most common problem with the R/T's DOHC four is blown head gaskets; that means owners need to stay on top of the cooling system to avoid overheating. There were also factory TSBs for broken valve springs, and the replacement of wheel bearings and various front-end bushings to cure an apparently common clunking sound. For a complete list of all Neon TSBs and recalls (plus a ton of other worthwhile tech, spec, and model info), visit www.neons.org. As with any overhead-cam engine, make sure the timing

The Neon R/T inline-four cranks out a most respectable 150 horsepower, which is impressive in that it doesn't employ any turbo or Honda/Acura VTEC-type technology. Early Neon engines were pretty noisy, but Dodge had really improved the car's overall NVH characteristics by the time the R/T model came along in 1998. The air intake tube is a nonstock item. *Matt Wiggins*

belts are replaced on schedule, and always make sure the front CV joint boots are in good condition.

The R/T would really benefit from a more aggressive, 15- or 16-inch wheel-and-tire package, easily found in the aftermarket. The aftermarket can also provide turbos, intake and exhaust systems, reprogrammed computers, and even more ardent suspension components. There's virtually no differences between the 1998 and 1999 cars except that 1999s have a newer-generation air bag system, and equipment availability was shuffled just a bit. Overall, a neat pocket rocket that's a ball to drive—for not a lot of money. Should help you save up for that Viper.

The R/T package seats befit a more expensive car, not so much in terms of the fabrics and materials used, which are about what you'd expect in a fairly low-cost machine, but because they are well bolstered and offer good side support too. And though we've shied away from sedans in this book, know that the R/T can also be had in four-door form, and the driving experience is virtually the same. *Matt Wiggins*

SPECIFICATIONS (1999 NEON R/T)

Body style . . . . Two door, five passenger
Drivetrain layout. . . . . Front engine, front drive
Engine type . . . . DOHC I-4
Displacement, liter/cc 2.0/1,996
Horsepower, hp @ rpm . . . . SAE net 150 @ 6,800
Torque, ft-lb @ rpm . . . . SAE net 131 @ 5,600
Transmission . . . . 5-speed manual
Wheelbase, in. 104.0
Length, in. 171.9
Width, in. 67.4
Height, in. 54.9
Base curb weight, lb 2,490
Suspension, f/r. . . . . MacPherson strut/Chapman strut and link
Steering type. . . . . Rack and pinion
Brakes, f/r. . . . . Disc/disc

PERFORMANCE

Acceleration, 0–60 mph, ... 8.5 sec.
Standing quarter
mile, sec/mph 16.4/87.3
Source . . . . Road & Track

TYPICAL PARTS/REPAIR PRICES

Major tune-up/service. $545
Air filter 5
Shock absorber 66
Catalytic converter(s) 98
Clutch replacement 700

WEBSITE

neons.org

Chapter 9

FOR
- Performance for the money
- Price/value ratio
- The original American pony car

AGAINST
- Slower than those dreaded Chevys
- Unsophisticated suspension
- Rear drum brakes on pre-1994s

HOT PICK
- 1993 LX 5.0, 1994/1995 SVT Cobra

REPORT CARD

Engine	A
Transmission	A
Power/Weight Ratio	A-
Handling	B
Braking	B-
Ride	B
Exterior Styling	B
Interior Styling	B
Interior Function	B+
Cargo Capacity	B
Everyday Usability	A-
Reliability	B
Fit and Finsh	B
Market Availability	A-
Resale Value Potential	B
Fun Factor	A-
Bang for Buck	A-
Aftermarket Interest	A
Club Support	A

Ford Mustang GT/LX 5.0 (1990–1998)

The term "bang for the buck" has been overused almost to the point of becoming meaningless. But if ever a car meant performance received for dollars invested, it's the Mustang of the 1990s. Mustang invented the pony car movement, beginning with the original 1964 -1/2 model, and remains amazingly true to its roots—that being rear-wheel drive, V-8-powered, and distinctly American.

Two basic series of Mustangs were built in the 1990s: the "Fox" platform cars of 1990–1993, and the "FOX4" machines (the platform was internally called SN95) of 1994–1998; 1999 and later Mustangs are based on a further update of the FOX4 design. By the time 1990 rolled around, the Fox-bodied Mustang had already been around more than a

Mustang enthusiasts are very split on whether the 1987–1993 Mustang is better than the later, "SN95" models of 1994–1998—but that's OK; Ford built plenty of both. The convertible is a 1996 SVT Cobra; the fastback is a 1991 LX 5.0.

LX 5.0 is a cleaner, slightly lighter design than the GT, though their mechanical specs are virtually identical. Five-star 16-inch wheels were new for 1991.

Naturally, the pre-1994 convertible used the rear clip and conventional trunk of the two-door sedan body style. The top looks good in an upright position, though it doesn't hide below the tonneau cover as neatly as some others.

decade—the 1979 model year to be exact. But beginning in 1982, the reintroduction of the much-missed Mustang GT led a return to musclecar performance that unquestionably saved the nameplate. The car received a thorough updating for the 1987 model year, and it remained in much the same form through 1993.

The real heart of any performance Mustang is its engine, and during these earlier years, all you needed to know was "5.0." The 5.0-liter V-8 traces its roots back to the V-8s found in those original 1960s Mustangs, but like Grandpa's axe, both the handle and the head had been changed so many times, it really wasn't the same thing anymore. While it was still an overhead valve design, it had been updated with modern fuel injection, roller-style camshaft and rockers, steel tube headers, and a true dual exhaust system. The result was 225 horsepower, and an absolutely impressive 300 ft-lb of torque. With 0–60 times in the 6.0-second range, it

was nearly as quick as certain Ferraris of the day, and nothing delivered more acceleration for the money.

Two transmissions were offered: a Borg-Warner T-5 5-speed manual or an optional four-speed automatic. While the automatic works fine and saps relatively little performance, the stick is the enthusiast's way to go. The horsepower rating actually dropped to 205 for 1993, but that was only due to the way the output was being measured, not due to any re-calibration of the engine.

Three body styles were offered: two-door fastback/hatchback, a two-door notchback coupe (the ones used by all those Highway Patrol departments), and a convertible. Each was available in two different performance trim levels, the GT and the LX. The GT is generally considered the top of the line, as it offered more aggressive bodywork (it's the one with the louver-style covers over the taillight) and integrated fog lights up

The two-door sedan model proved an exceptionally popular law enforcement vehicle: it's tough, fast, and reasonably priced. The California Highway Patrol began using 5.0-powered Mustangs in 1982; this is one of the last 1993 models.

A cutaway chassis rendering of the new-for-1994 SN95-bodied Mustang. Note the overhead-cam engine in this 1996. *David Kimball, courtesy Ford*

front. However, the same powertrains and suspension tuning were offered in LX trim, as this is the one that has actually found more favor with the Mustang performance set. The LX sported less-adorned bodywork, so some felt it actually looked more modern. It cost less, and more importantly, it weighed less, so an LX was usually a tick or two quicker through the lights than a comparably equipped GT.

While the 5.0 powertrain drivetrain is a thing of wonder, you can feel the car's late-1970s heritage in other areas. All of these Mustangs feature a live rear axle—not known as being the hot ticket for maximum handling and a smooth ride. And with few exceptions, they all had rear drum brakes and no ABS; adequate, but not really up to the car's acceleration potential. There were rela-

tively few changes from 1990 to 1993; a driver-side air bag and a step up to 16-inch wheels came along in 1991, and the aforementioned horsepower rating drop in 1993. These cars don't offer the handling sophistication, fit, or finish level you'll find in a Honda Prelude or BMW 3 Series of the same era, but they sure do go.

Ford offered a few "special edition" packages during this era: a monochromatic yellow convertible for 1993, a similar all-white version for 1992, etc. Some sellers attempt to portray these as some sort of collectible, and price the cars accordingly. It's our opinion that since these models didn't offer performance or any special equipment beyond a standard Mustang—save for a color scheme—they are not worth any additional money.

When Ford launched its new Mustang in 1994, it reconciled the model lineup from three body styles to two; the previous hatchback design went away, and even the fastback coupe had a conventional trunk. This was done in the name of a structurally stiff chassis, and made things simpler on the production line too. *Ford*

Most of the changes for 1996 aren't visible from the outside, but the 4.6 GT badge on the side signaled the last appearance for the venerable 5.0-liter small-block V-8. The front end received a subtle grille that later proved to inhibit airflow, so it was dumped for 1997. This car has the standard 16-inch alloy wheels. *Ford*

This 1997 GT sports the Mustang's optional 17-inch wheels and tire package, which really sharpens steering response and ultimate grip, due to the wider 245-section tires. These 1996–1998 wheel designs are also a lot nicer looking than the spindly "tri-spoke" wheels found on the 1994–1995 GTs.

Nineteen ninety-four brought a substantial overhaul. While there were some carryover chassis components, everything you could see or touch was new. Ford reconciled the lineup from three body styles to two: a fastback coupe with trunk and a convertible. No more hatchbacks. Much to the chagrin of many a weekend racer, the LX model also left town. All GTs were V-8s and visa versa, with base-model Mustangs now powered by a 3.8-liter V-6 of 145–150 horsepower.

The chassis was substantially strengthened (better handling, better ride, fewer creaks and squeaks), and equipment levels were increased. All Mustangs now packed four-wheel disc brakes, with ABS as an option. A new dual-cockpit interior design boasted dual front air bags, and an optional Mach 460 sound system that was just about as good as any factory-offered system in its day, and still sounds excellent today.

V-8 drivetrains essentially carried over, though slightly different heads and intake hardware adjusted the horsepower rating to 215. The new car weighed a tad more, and performance dropped a bit, but the essential flavor was retained, and the new Mustang was a much more sophisticated car overall. Save for minor tweaks, the Mustang remained in this form for the 1994 and 1995 model years.

Nineteen ninety-six brought only minor updates on the outside but big changes under the hood. A few years before, Ford had introduced a new, more-modern engine family of single-overhead cam and dual-overhead cam V-8s that were headed the Mustang's way as soon as they could make enough of them. The new 4.6-liter SOHC V-8 first appeared in 1996 Mustang GTs. Although displacement decreased, the horsepower rating remained the same, despite offering slightly less torque. These engines, which feature alloy heads and a newer-generation engine management system, are smoother than the old 5.0-liters, and rev about 1,000 rpms higher.

Opinion among the Mustang faithful is split on which is really preferable. Some like the 1994–1995 cars, as they offer the benefits of the new chassis and body combined with the displacement as easy performance gains to be had from the trusty 5.0. Others like the revvier nature, more modern design, and increased fuel mileage of the overhead cam V-8s.

Physical changes were few: the horizontal taillight theme of the 1994–1995 cars gave way to a more

Specialist constructor Saleen has made its trade building limited-edition, high-performance Mustangs. Some are rare, with 351-ci engines and/or superchargers, and are not likely to slip into the sub-$20K price range anytime soon. But others, like the more common S-281 models, might be had for that.

Ford really upgraded the interior of the Mustang for 1994–1998; this dual cockpit look features dual air bags, a CD player, and an optional Mach 460 top-line stereo system, none of which could be had on the previous-generation car. *Ford*

The 1990–1993 Mustang dash design had been around since the remodel for 1987. Though not exactly swoopy, it got the job done. This is a 1991 or later car, as evidenced by the driver's-side-only airbag; leather was also available from that year on. It's hard to beat Ford's placement of the cruise control buttons on the steering wheel. The engine gauge pack replacing the center dash vents is an aftermarket piece.

attractive vertical three-light design, and there were new alloy wheels. Again you could choose between a standard five-speed stick or a four-speed automatic.

In addition to the standard model offerings, Ford launched its exclusive roster of SVT models, beginning in 1993. SVT stands for Special Vehicle Team, an enthusiast-model planning, engineering, and marketing group within Ford. SVT's goal is to build enhanced performance versions of existing Ford models, and an SVT Mustang Cobra has been a part of the lineup since the beginning. The approach is somewhat similar as taken with BMW's M models or an AMG Mercedes: offer a hotter motor, more luxurious interior, better handling, subtle visual distinction from the standard models, and limited production.

The first 1993 SVT Cobra was built during the Fox platform's last year on the market, and thus has become somewhat collectible. It packs a 240-horsepower 5.0-liter, four-wheel disc brakes, monochromatic paint, aggressive rocker panels and rear wing, revised suspension, and 17-inch Z-rated rolling stock. The 1993 SVT Cobra certainly represents the zenith of 1979–1993 Mustang factory development.

The Cobra continued through 1994 and 1995 (initially only in coupe form, though convertibles soon followed), though there were less visual changes: a revised front air dam and rear wing, and Cobra-specific 17-inch wheels, brakes and suspension tuning. White-faced gauges became an SVT trademark, and the 240-horsepower OHV powertrain carried over. No automatic trans was offered. The SVT Cobra served as the Indy 500 Pace Car, and there are a few red commemorative Indy Pace Car street versions around too.

These SN95, 5.0-powered Cobras are great buys if you can find a good one.

Nothing makes a car more special than a special engine, and the SVT Cobra certainly got one for 1996. Although still 4.6 liters, the all-new Cobra V-8 was a hand-assembled double-overhead cam, four-valve-per-cylinder powerplant rated at 305 horsepower and 300 ft-lb of torque. This all-aluminum powerplant is only too happy to rev to its 7,000-rpm redline, and adds the measure of sophistication that SVT strives for.

You may have also heard of a street/race version called the Cobra R. Exactly 107 Cobra Rs were built in 1993, with another 250 for 1995. This model was developed to compete in several race classes, and was sold primarily to those with competition licenses, and of course, Mustang collectors. They remain way outside our price range.

All 1990s Mustangs are relatively sturdy cars. The engines are virtually bulletproof, a good thing as enthusiastic owners tend to drive them accordingly. 5.0s will tend to start using oil at around 80,000 miles, but otherwise are usually good to 120,000 miles-plus. Clutches can last up to 100,000 miles, but only if driven moderately. The manual transmissions are tough, too, though second gear and other synchros will wear out under abusive treatment. No problem, however, as even a brand-new transmission is not an expensive proposition.

Interior materials don't fare nearly as well; a Mustang that spends much time in the sun invariably has a cracked upper dash panel, and seat fabrics begin showing wear after only a few years. The factory shock absorbers don't usually last long either, though any Mustang's handling can be improved by the installation of higher performance shocks (and by the way, the rear axle on 1990–1993 cars use four shocks). Convertible tops, particularly on the 1990–1993s, don't last long either, though those on the later cars seem to fare better. 1990–1993 cars tend to get "rattly" with age, though there are easily installed chassis-stiffening braces available from the aftermarket (see below); later cars are not affected by this situation.

Part of the Mustang's appeal is that it's supported by a large and active aftermarket. As with most Hondas and VWs, there are lots of pieces and parts available to make your Mustang into anything you want it to be. Supercharged engines putting out 500 horsepower, and Mustangs packing sophisticated, Porsche-killing suspensions, are not uncommon. There are wild body kits, aggressive wheel/tire/brake combinations, you name it.

If you want to have a car you can fiddle with and modify in the true American hot rodding tradition, can appreciate rear-wheel drive and the burble of eight cylinders, and can overlook a few rough edges as compared to some of the premium German and Japanese offerings, a 1990s-era Mustang is as good a pick as they come. Like we said: bang for buck.

SPECIFICATIONS (1996 MUSTANG GT)

Body style	Two door, five passenger
Drivetrain layout	Front engine, front drive
Engine type	SOHC V-8
Displacement, liter/cc	4.6/4,601
Horsepower, hp @ rpm	SAE net 215 @ 4,400
Torque, ft-lb @ rpm	SAE net 285 @ 3,500
Transmission	5-speed manual
Wheelbase, in.	101.3
Length, in.	181.5
Width, in.	71.8
Height, in.	53.2
Base curb weight, lb	3,410
Suspension, f/r	MacPherson strut/live axle
Steering type	Rack and pinion
Brakes, f/r	Disc/disc

PERFORMANCE

Acceleration, 0–60 mph	6.8 sec.
Standing quarter mile, sec/mph	15.3/89.0
Source	Road & Track

TYPICAL PARTS/REPAIR PRICES

Major tune-up/service	$375
Air filter	8
Shock absorber	58
Catalytic converter(s)	277
Clutch replacement	675

WEBSITES

mustang.org
mustang-unl.com
saleen.com

REPORT CARD

Engine	B
Transmission	B
Power/Weight Ratio	B
Handling	B+
Braking	B-
Ride	B
Exterior Styling	B
Interior Styling	B
Interior Function	B+
Cargo Capacity	B+
Everyday Usability	A-
Reliability	B
Fit and Finish	A-
Market Availability	C+
Resale Value Potential	C
Fun Factor	B
Bang for Buck	B-
Aftermarket Interest	C
Club Support	C

Ford Probe GT (1993–1997)

The Ford Probe is one of those cars that deserved better. It began life in the mid-1980s as a design study to replace the rear-wheel-drive Mustang with a more modern, front-wheel-drive platform. When the Mustang faithful went berserk (rightfully so—American musclecars have rear-wheel drive and V-8 engines, period!), Ford was too far along to dump the project. So they continued its development, copped the name Probe from a Ford race car, and figured they'd sell it alongside the Mustang. The original Probe appeared as a 1989 model, and this first-generation platform continued through the 1992 model year.

So why are we starting this chapter with the 1993 model? It's just a more modern, capable platform all the way around. Although the early car has a certain following, there really isn't much in the way of aftermarket or performance potential for it, and the styling—inside and out—is looking decidedly 1980s. The newer Probe has more potential and appeal, yet costs little more to buy and own.

The new-for-1993 Ford Probe was one of the more recent cars to successfully incorporate pop-up headlights into its design, and most began switching to glass-enclosed lights in the early 1990s. The V-6-powered GT model is easily distinguished by its fog lamps and 16-inch wheels. *Ford*

This Ford PR photo must have been taken well in advance of the 1994 model's appearance, as nobody we've spoken to has ever seen a Probe with these body-colored wheels. *Ford*

The second-generation Probe was a joint development project between Ford and Mazda; the Mazda product was called the MX-6. To look at them, you'd never know they were cousins beneath the sheet metal, so different are their styling treatments. The Probe is certainly edgier, racier, and though they shared power-trains and suspension systems, the Probe received more aggressive suspension tuning and rolling stock. Most of our commentary about the Probe goes for the MX-6 too; if you like its swoopy, decidedly European styling treatment and don't object to its slightly softer suspension settings, there's no reason not to consider one. They tend to be a bargain—as like the Probe, the MX-6 is no longer in the lineup. The probe was offered in two distinct models, each with its own power-train. The base Probe came with a 115-horsepower 2.0-liter DOHC four, and the buyer's choice of a four-speed automatic or five-speed manual transmission.

The enthusiast will want to head straight for the Probe GT, the main reason being its 2.5-liter 164-horse-power DOHC V-6. This all-alloy, double-overhead cam V-6 is a Mazda unit, and is nothing less than a jewel. It's quite smooth, revs happily, and sounds great doing so. While it lacks a bit of torque in the lower rev ranges (though it's still stronger down low than most fours), it's an engine you won't mind revving a bit to make the most of. Buyers again had the choice of a standard five-speed manual transmission or an optional four-speed automatic. We've driven both, and while the five-speed

is the obvious performance choice, the automatic's ratios are well matched to the engine's power band and seems to sap fairly little out of the V-6.

Suspension is a fully independent layout, with MacPherson struts up front and a multilink setup in back. Disc/drum brake combinations were still quite the norm in mid-1992 when the second-gen Probe was introduced, but the GT model got power-assisted four-wheel discs, and ABS was optional. GT rolling stock consisted of 16x7.0-inch alloy wheels, and 225-50VR16 performance tires; again, pretty aggressive stuff for the day, and the original five-spoke alloys still look good today.

Inside, the Probe is sporty and comfortable, if perhaps a bit cramped for the tallest of drivers. If it weren't for the lack of things like a passenger-side air bag and a dozen cup holders, you'd take it for a much newer car. Instrumentation is thankfully complete, and easy to read. Standard equipment on the GT included power rack-and-pinion steering, the afore-mentioned power four-wheel disc brakes, an AM/FM stereo, leather-wrapped steering wheel, and fog lamps.

The Probe GT offered goodies like air condition-ing, ABS, an anti-theft system, several sound systems including a graphic equalizer and single-play CD, power windows and seats, leather seating surfaces, sport seats, cruise control, and a power sunroof. Most cars we've inspected seem to be equipped with most of these items.

Swan song: 1997 was the Probe's final year on the market; front fascia is slightly different than on earlier cars, and chrome wheels are also of a different design. Otherwise, the Probe changed relatively little during its five-year run. *Ford*

Perhaps knowing that the Mustang would be revised again for 1994 (and later for 1999), plus the introduction of a new, but philosophically similar Mercury Cougar (also for 1999), development of the Probe was kept to a minimum during its five-year model run. For 1994, Ford jumped all over the Probe's seating situation: the optional leather trim was deleted, as was the sport seat option. So were some of the power adjustment controls—so somewhere along the way, Ford decided to go with a wholly cheaper seat design and supplier. Nothing wrong with them, but leather seats have only gotten more popular, not less. Option groups were slightly revised, one new color was added, as was a passenger-side air bag.

After just two years on the market, the Probe got a minor freshening. An SE model was added between the base and GT versions, though it was just a slightly tarted-up four-cylinder car; the GT remained the sportiest version. While the sizes remained the same, the GT's five-spoke wheel was of a new design and could also be ordered in chrome finish. Taillights were revised, and the GT's rear end redesign included a center trim panel between the taillamp assemblies and a revised bumper cover. Inside, the console was

redone, and a second cup holder was added. There were new seat fabrics restyled interior door panels, and both interior and exterior color combinations were shuffled. No other functional performance hardware was affected.

Minor revisions also came in 1996. Option packages, colors, and fabrics received minor tweaking. Remote fuel and hatch releases were made standard on all models. There was one dynamic change that may or may not be a good thing, depending on your preferences: suspension settings, including spring rates and shock valving, were softened in the name of an improved ride. While Ford claims that the Probe's handling wasn't compromised, owners have told me the 1996 is indeed a slightly softer car. There's no doubt that freeway ride improved a bit, but perhaps at the expense of a bit of the Probe's sharp-edged handling. Aftermarket shocks, and perhaps a more aggressive 17-inch wheel-and-tire package, would probably bring things back into line, and perhaps even yield an increase over the 1993–1995 Probe's handling abilities.

For its swan-song year of 1997, little was changed. The GT received new badging (for some reason), and equipment option packages were again reshuffled to

The Probe's interior looks very fresh for a car that came out in 1993. The wraparound dash orients nicely toward the driver, though we sure miss the grippier sport seats that came in the first-year cars. The door pockets are wide, and cruise controls on the steering wheel are certainly handy. Ford did a decent job of integrating this optional CD sound system with graphic EQ, even if there are a considerable number of similarly sized buttons that are sure to cause some confusion until the driver gets used to their functions. *Ford*

make them more attractively priced. Leather seats were once again optional, two new colors were added, and unfortunately, that would be that.

We can't recommend one specific year over another; some feel the 1993, with its firmer suspension and sport seat option, was the best, though the older the car, the more miles its likely to have. It's probably possible to find late 1996 and 1997 cars in good condition with relatively low miles. The Probe is one of those cars where the condition, color, transmission, and equipment of a particular example are more important than a specific year or model. It was ostensibly the same car during all five model years.

A common problem seems to be brake noise, caused by the factory pads. Owners have recommended using high-quality aftermarket pads, and say it cures the problem. Clutches are good for about 80,000 miles; plan on replacing on any car with more miles than that, if it hasn't been done already. Like most multi-cam engines, timing belts need to be replaced; that service interval on the Probe's V-6 is 60,000 miles, and if an owner can't provide a receipt for the work, negotiate on the price and get the job done immediately (about $300). The automatic transmission seems to be a tough piece, causing no particular problems. Factory shocks seem to wear out in as little as 30,000 miles, a good time to upgrade to higher quality aftermarket units. Otherwise, the Probe has proven to be a relatively trouble-free piece, and if you don't mind driving a model no longer on the market, makes an excellent-driving, V-6 sports coupe buy.

SPECIFICATIONS (1995 PROBE GT)

Body style . . . . Two door, five passenger
Drivetrain layout. . . . . Front engine, front drive
Engine type . . . . DOHC V-6
Displacement, liter/cc 2.5/2,497
Horsepower, hp @ rpm . . . . SAE net 164 @ 5,600
Torque, ft-lb @ rpm . . . . SAE net 160 @ 4,800
Transmission . . . . 5-speed manual
Wheelbase, in. 102.9
Length, in. 178.0
Width, in.. . . . . 69.8
Height, in. 51.9
Base curb weight, lb 3,000
Suspension, f/r. . . . . MacPherson strut/Chapman strut, link
Steering type. . . . . Rack and pinion
Brakes, f/r . . . . Disc/disc

PERFORMANCE

Acceleration, 0–60 mph . . . . 7.9 sec.
Standing quarter
mile, sec/mph 16.0/87.5
Source . . . . Road & Track

TYPICAL PARTS/REPAIR PRICES

Major tune-up/service. $360
Air filter 12
Shock absorber 62
Catalytic converter(s) 82
Clutch replacement 925

WEBSITE

fortunecity.com/silverstone/tyre/801

Honda CRX
(1990–1991)

When the first Honda CRX came out as a 1984 model, you could hear the sports car traditionalists scream: "*Real* sports cars don't have front-wheel drive!" or "The tops go down on *real* sports cars!" And finally, "Japanese car companies don't know how to make a good cheap sports car." Well—guess what: the CRX is *absolutely* a sports car, and a reasonably inexpensive one at that. It has since garnered a positively huge cult following—even though it's been out of production since 1991.

Like the first-generation models (1984–1987), the second-generation CRX (actually 1988-1991) was based on the then-current Civic platform. That was a good thing even then, as Honda's reputation for sporty underpinnings, solid build quality, and reliability were already well established. Even though this book focuses on cars built in 1990 or later, our comments apply to the largely identical 1988–1999 model CRXs as well, and there's no reason not to consider an earlier vehicle.

The front-drive, hatchback, two-seater CRX was offered in three models: the fuel-stingy HF model, the "standard" DX, and the performance-oriented Si. The HF (for High Fuel economy), while still a CRX,

Considering the CRX's humble Civic platform, it made a most successful transition to two-seat sports car. These second-gen CRXs also look more squat and substantial than the earlier models. *James Brown*

One of the more unusual aspects of the CRX's basically straightforward design is the use of a vertical glass panel on the rear deck. This was because the main rear window was sloped so steeply that rear visibility was unacceptable. So, the rear glass panel enhanced the view out from the rearview mirror. *James Brown*

is saddled with a 1.5-liter, two-valve-per-cylinder SOHC four good for just 62 horsepower. The HF was available only with a five-speed manual transmission. It also had the lowest levels of interior trimmings, the least performance-oriented suspension, and very high gear ratios to further aid fuel economy. Unless you really want any CRX, plan to do extensive modifications, or find one in perfect condition at an absolute giveaway price, enthusiasts should avoid this model.

DXs are a bit more desirable, with better interior trim and equipment levels, and most importantly, a four-valve-per-cylinder, throttle-body fuel-injected SOHC four putting out a more sporting 92 horsepower (which still doesn't sound like a lot, but the CRX's light chassis helps its power-to-weight ratio). DXs could be had with your choice of a five-speed manual or an optional automatic transmission, the only CRX so offered.

The connoisseur's choice among CRXs is the Si model, which packed a 1.6-liter, four-valves-per-cylinder multi-port fuel-injected four cranking out 105 horsepower, certainly impressive for the times. Along

Those 14-inch alloys don't look so tough on many cars these days, but still look good on the pint-sized CRX. We've seen modified cars around on 16s and even 17s, and they also look great—if you don't go overboard on tire/wheel selection. *James Brown*

Like the rest of the CRX, the interior is simple, yet well done. There's plenty of legroom for even the tallest drivers, though the cabin only holds two. And not an air bag in sight. *James Brown*

with it came sportier suspension tuning, standard alloy wheels, a sliding glass sunroof, a lower-front air dam, and other sporty accouterments. An Si in good condition commands a healthy premium over HF and DX models, but the enhanced performance will be worth it to buyers who want the "ultimate" CRX.

All CRXs offered quick and sporty feeling rack-and-pinion steering, power front disc brakes (with rear discs standard on 1990–1991 models), electronic ignitions, and of course that innovative glass panel at the base of the rear deck. One of the main reasons CRXs—and most Hondas—handle so well is the use of double A-arm suspension systems front and rear. Most inexpensive front drivers use the more cost-effective MacPherson struts up front, and some sort of beam axle out back. But the wishbone setups allow low fender lines and maintain more constant camber settings, which aid handling. They cost more but are part of what gives the CRX true sports car credentials.

This hails from the days before high-powered stereos and built-in CD players, so this is one area almost any CRX buyer will want to consider upgrading. Also keep in mind that the CRX does not have some of the latest safety features, such as air bags or ABS brakes, though this has certainly not dimmed their appeal.

There were relatively few changes during "Series 2" CRXs life. The Si model was re-rated at 108 horsepower for 1989. 1990 brought subtle front sheetmetal tweaks, revised taillights, the aforementioned standard rear disc brakes, and larger, easier-to-read gauges. 1991 was a carryover; given the slightly

updated look and improved brakes, the 1990–1991 cars are considered the most desirable, but not by so much that a well-maintained, low-mileage 1988 or 1989 should be ignored.

CRXs were not plagued by any chronic problems, but like most cars, need to be regularly maintained to avoid becoming money pits. Fortunately, parts and service are plentiful. Most critical are timely replacements of the timing belt; though Honda says it needs to be done each 90,000 miles, these have been known to break, and experts recommend more like a 60,000-mile replacement schedule.

Honda engines are well built and love to rev, but that also means they burn down engine oil more often than others. An oil and filter change every 3,000–5,000 miles is smarter than the factory-recommended 7,500. A high-revving engine in the hands of a ham-fisted driver is also hard on the clutch assembly, so make sure it is smooth, and the engagement is somewhere near the middle of the pedal travel. CV joints also have a tendency to go bad, so whining and growling from the front end may indicate these units have had it. Rather than just replacing the CV joints, many CRX owners recommend simply replacing the entire half-shaft, which includes both joints. Figure $125 per side, plus installation. A clunking sound in the front end usually means a worn steering rack; new ones run about $250 plus labor. A clunking/groaning noise about back is caused by a worn rear trailing arm bushing—no big deal. There were also several factory technical service bulletins issued concerning the DX's

Small, but, well—relatively mighty. Even though the 1.6-Si motor was no powerhouse, the CRX benefited from a reasonable power-to-weight ratio. How 'bout swapping in a later VTEC motor? It's been done, but unfortunately, we've not driven one. *James Brown*

automatic transmission (seal problems, leaks, etc.), but most CRX owners probably want the five-speeders anyway.

The CRX, as with most Civics and Civic-based machines, is one of those cars that owners just love to modify, so all of the issues we discussed at the beginning of this book apply. But if a lightweight screamer is what you want, the CRX is a great candidate: turbos, later VTEC engines (be careful about registration and local smog requirements, however), performance suspensions, and high-tech rolling stock. Honda may have one of the world's most fervent aftermarket fol-lowings, and you can really make these cars perform. Check out some of the websites, and see what owners have done to their cars.

Although the del Sol technically replaced the CRX in Honda's lineup (it was actually badged a CRX in certain world markets), it was really a different beast altogether. Many CRX owners never warmed to the round headlight, notchback, and targa-topped styling, and the del Sol is a larger, heavier, more sophisticated, and more expensive vehicle. Ask CRX aficionados when the last real CRX was made, and they'll tell you 1991. And they're still waiting for a new one.

SPECIFICATIONS (1991 CRX Si)

Body style	Two door, two passenger
Drivetrain layout	Front engine, front drive
Engine type	SOHC I-4
Displacement, liter/cc	1.6/1,590
Horsepower, hp @ rpm	SAE net 108 @ 6,000
Torque, ft-lb @ rpm	SAE net 100 @ 5,000
Transmission	5-speed manual
Wheelbase, in.	90.6
Length, in.	148.5
Width, in.	65.9
Height, in.	50.1
Base curb weight, lb	2,115
Suspension, f/r	Upper and lower A-arms/upper and lower A-arms
Steering type	Rack and pinion
Brakes, f/r	Disc/disc

PERFORMANCE

Acceleration, 0–60 mph	8.9 sec.
Standing quarter mile, sec/mph	17.1/83.0
Source	Road & Track

TYPICAL PARTS/REPAIR PRICES

Major tune-up/service	$330
Air filter	11
Shock absorber	66
Catalytic converter(s)	162
Clutch replacement	780

WEBSITES

crx.org
geocities.com/Athens/3966/crx/crxring.html
honda-acura.net
hondaclub.com

Honda Civic Si (1999)

REPORT CARD

Engine	A
Transmission	B+
Power/Weight Ratio	A-
Handling	A-
Braking	B+
Ride	B
Exterior Styling	B+
Interior Styling	B+
Interior Function	A-
Cargo Capacity	B+
Everyday Usability	A
Reliability	A
Fit and Finish	A
Market Availability	B
Resale Value Potential	A-
Fun Factor	A-
Bang for Buck	A
Aftermarket Interest	A
Club Support	A

Honda's remarkably successful Civic has been called "the '57 Chevy of the 1990s." Strange, but true. For its day, the 1955–1957 Chevrolet set new standards for performance, quality, value, and all-around goodness. They also became the modern-day darlings for those seeking high performance in a new car at a reasonable price. These "Tri-Year Chevys" were appreciated by housewife and racer alike, and the latter began modifying them as quickly as they could roll them off show-room floors. Much the same can be said of Ford's original Mustang of the mid-1960s.

And so it is with the Civic: a high-volume, economy compact that has also caught the eye of the youthful enthusiast. Pick up a copy of *Sport Compact Car* or *Super Street* magazines, and you'll understand the phenom. But for some strange reason, Honda waited until 1999 to itself capitalize on the Civic's latent performance potential. Actually, when you analyze Honda's mid-1990s lineup, it's a bit easier to understand

Finally, the souped-up Civic that everyone knew Honda could build and sell, yet never did. Yes, there were previous Civics badged as Si models that had a somewhat less sophisticated version of the VTEC engine, but it took until 1999 for Honda to deliver it all in one package. *Honda*

We've seen some pretty gaudy, poorly designed body kits on Civics, but fortunately, Honda resisted the urge to get to crazy with the Si's styling; just a mild front fascia redo, a bit less chrome, and subtly redone rocker panels give it just enough extra attitude. *Honda*

why they waited: there was always some other platform awaiting the high-tech hardware, be it the del Sol two-seater or the upmarket Acura Integra. But Honda did finally jump on its own aftermarket-driven band-wagon, and the result is the Civic Si.

The hot rod Civic Si was introduced as a 1999 model and offered but one body style, the two-door coupe. Honda's approach to tweaking more out of the Civic is much the same as BMW would do to an M model: improve, by somewhat equal measure, levels of acceleration, braking, handling, luxury, and give it all a businesslike, performance-oriented appearance.

Powering the Si is a 1.6-liter four that, although it shares the same size and architecture with Honda's standard 1.6, is really a much-upgraded beast. Most of the power increase comes via Honda's VTEC system, which means variable timing and lift for the valves; the goal is to preserve low-end torque, and then switch (at 5,500 rpm) to more aggressive cam timing for high rpm work. The intake manifold, exhaust, and engine management systems are tuned accordingly. The result

is an increase from the standard 127 horsepower to a more-notable 160 horses. That may not sound like a big number, but its impressive for 1.6-liters; note that the VW Beetle Turbo employs a larger 1.8-liter engine and a turbocharger—all to get 10-less horsepower than the Si. The only transmission available is a five-speed manual, and you'll use every gear to enjoy the Si engine's 8,000-rpm redline.

Suspension-wise, the Si gets stiffer front springs, firmer shock absorber valving, and it's lowered just a bit compared to the standard Civic coupe. Larger 15-inch wheels also help in the handling department, and the Si's monochrome paint scheme adds additional performance flavor. The front fascia is also a bit more aggressive, and the final performance-related bit of hardware is the switch from the standard disc/drum setup to four-wheel discs (though curiously, no ABS system is offered).

While $18,000 or so may sound like a lot for a Civic, it's an exceptional performance value for the money, in fact, one that qualified for inclusion in this

Owners should resist the urge to toss these factory 15-inch alloys in the trash, and "slam" the Civic Si to the ground. It's a very competent handler just the way it comes from the factory. OK, maybe some nice 16s, but go easy with those lowering kits. *Honda*

With the exception of some leather trim on the shift knob and steering wheel, and more thickly bolstered seats, the Si interior is stock Civic. But that's a good thing, as materials are of high quality, fit, and finish is as good as you'll find, and the overall ergonomics are sound. Seat fabric is grippy, and appears durable. *Honda*

book as a brand-new car. The Si is a hoot to drive, though it may take a bit of getting used to for drivers who were born and raised on torque. The VTEC's torque peak is only 111 ft-lb, and it arrives at a lofty 7,000 rpm. So just think of it as a four-wheel motorcycle, work the engine in VTEC mode (5,500 revs to redline), and you'll get the most out of it.

The rest of the package is delightful, explaining why the Civic, even in base form, is so popular. The seats are firm and comfortable, visibility is excellent, and the car begs to be driven (hard). It's a rewarding

handler, too, even with what seem like rather average 15-inch alloy wheels and tires—sort of makes you wonder why so many people fit 17-inch, 18-inch, and even larger wheels to their Civics. Strictly vanity, at some point. For example, the Civic Si bested the Dodge Neon, VW Jetta GLX, Ford Escort ZX2, and the Hyundai Tiburon in a slalom handling performance test conducted by *AutoWeek*. So the hardware works.

Fit, finish, and materials quality are outstanding, something we've come to expect from Honda, and considering the somewhat-limited production nature of the Si, we suspect it will be one to hold its value well. The Si is a one-price-buys-all model, with virtually no options, but any interior color you want—so long as it's gray. Civics have proven to be exceptionally reliable, with no notable weak points, but there are a few things to watch out for. As noted, it takes revs to get the most out of the Si's high-strung powerplant. So, records of frequent oil changes and an owner who took the time to warm up the car before venturing toward redline will go a long way toward maximizing engine life. And considering that an Si owner shouldn't hesitate to drive the car aggressively, clutches and transmissions can suffer from the abuse of a ham-fisted driver. If the car you're considering has over 60,000 miles on it, find out if the timing belt has ever been replaced, and if not, consider that into the cost of the car. Grumbling noises from the front end probably indicate worn CV joints. A thorough driveline inspection is important when contemplating the used Si. Otherwise, it should be viewed as any other Civic, and

Detail of the gas and temperature gauge shows how Honda badged the top with the red "Si." *Honda*

given reasonable care, should lead a long and relatively trouble-free life.

As discussed in relation to other Honda models, the Civic is supported by an amazingly fervent aftermarket. No other Japanese brand, with the possible exception of the Mitsubishi Eclipse or perhaps the Mazda Miata, enjoys such an ardent following among young performance enthusiasts. Several companies make nothing other than Honda performance accessories; there are also clubs, dozens of Honda-only websites, and even Honda/Acura marque magazines. So you have the option of cranking even more performance and/or handling out of your Si (or any Civic) if you wish.

SPECIFICATIONS (1999 HONDA CIVIC Si)

Body style . . . . Two door, five passenger
Drivetrain layout. . . . . Front engine, front drive
Engine type . . . . DOHC I-4
Displacement, liter/cc 1.6/1,598
Horsepower, hp @ rpm . . . . SAE net 160 @ 7,600
Torque, ft-lb @ rpm . . . . SAE net 111 @ 7,000
Transmission . . . . 5-speed manual
Wheelbase, in. 103.2
Length, in. 175.1
Width, in. 67.1
Base curb weight, lb 2,601
Suspension, f/r. . . . . Double A-arm/double A-arm
Steering type. . . . . Rack and pinion
Brakes, f/r. . . . . Disc/disc

PERFORMANCE

Acceleration, 0–60 mph . . . . 7.2 sec.
Standing quarter
mile, sec/mph 15.6/88.9
Source . . . . AutoWeek

TYPICAL PARTS/REPAIR PRICES

Major tune-up/service. $500
Air filter 9
Shock absorber 84
Catalytic converter(s) 86
Clutch replacement 820

WEBSITES

hondaclub.com
honda-acura.net

Chapter 13

Honda Civic del Sol (1993–1997)

FOR
- High-tech demi-convertible body style
- Screaming 160-horse engine in VTEC form
- Double-wishbone suspension

AGAINST
- Not everyone likes the style
- Some parts getting hard to come by
- Not a spiritual successor to much missed CRX

HOT PICK
1995–1997 del Sol VTEC

REPORT CARD

Engine	A-
Transmission	B
Power/Weight Ratio	A-
Handling	A-
Braking	B+
Ride	B-
Exterior Styling	C
Interior Styling	B
Interior Function	B-
Cargo Capacity	C+
Everyday Usability	B
Reliability	A-
Fit and Finish	A-
Market Availability	B
Resale Value Potential	B
Fun Factor	B
Bang for Buck	A-
Aftermarket Interest	A
Club Support	A

Honda's cult sports car, the CRX, was a tough act to follow. So the company elected to change directions a bit: the Civic del Sol (which loosely translates to "of the sun") features a Porsche Targa-style removable roof panel, where the CRX is a coupe. And while the CRX is a fastback/hatchback, the del Sol offers a conventional trunk. The Civic del Sol is larger and wider, sharing its platform with the new-for-1992 Civic. Its styling doesn't resemble the CRX in any way.

The del Sol's (the Civic badge was removed beginning in 1995) big selling point is the removable roof panel, certainly an appealing notion in a sports car, and an alternative to a conventional folding fabric roof. Its relatively lightweight (24 pounds) roof panel stows neatly in the trunk, and there's still 8.3 cubic feet of trunk space left when the top is stored. Credit Honda for stiffening the chassis to minimize cowl shake, and wind buffeting is reasonably well controlled. Another fact that sets the del Sol (and indeed most Hondas) ahead of many of its

While the del Sol's styling wasn't as inspired as the previous CRX, it was a different kind of car. It was also hard to argue with the Si's 125-horsepower, the VTEC's 160-horses, and the appeal of its open-air transformability. This is a 1994 Si, though it looked virtually identical to the VTEC model. *Honda*

The del Sol's rear roof buttress somewhat resembles that of the early-1970s Porsche 914, though that midengine machine didn't have the del's power rear window, which further enhanced the almost-a-convertible experience. *Honda*

competitors is the use of a true double-wishbone suspension system front and rear; this allows the wheels to maintain caster and camber settings throughout the suspension's travel for more consistent handling. Most cars in this class, especially front drivers, use cheaper MacPherson struts up front, and some sort of beam axle out back, neither of which is nearly as sophisticated as the Honda systems.

Upon launch for the 1993 model year, two del Sol models were offered: the S, with a fairly pedestrian 1.5-liter 102-horsepower four, and the Si, with a 1.6-liter 125-horsepower four with variable valve timing. The former should be considered as purely an economy model, and won't do much for the driving enthusiast. The 125-horse Si is better, but the performance model that everyone waited for came along for 1994: the del Sol VTEC.

Honda's VTEC system (Variable valve Timing and lift Electronic Control) is a sophisticated variable valve timing system that manages both the intake and exhaust side of the head to provide good low-end torque and increased top-end power. At approximately 5,500 rpm, higher spec camshaft lobes take over control of the valves, giving these engines amazing top-end power. The driver can even hear the VTEC system switching to the higher cam spec as you rev past 5,500. The result is 160 horsepower at 7,600 rpm, and the 1.6-liter VTEC four is also a higher-revving DOHC design, as opposed to the single-overhead cam engines in the S and Si models. Additionally, all 1994 models received a standard passenger-side air bag (1993s had only a driver-side bag), so unless you find the world's nicest 1993 Si at a bargain price, we recommend a 1994 or later car, with the VTEC being the obvious performance choice.

VTEC models also received a close-ratio five-speed manual transmission; only the S and Si could be had with a four-speed automatic. For some reason, these proved troublesome as installed in del Sols and are best avoided. The suspension was also upgraded for VTEC model duty, with larger tires, and anti-roll bars front and rear. Quicker ratio power rack-and-pinion steering, four-wheel disc brakes, power windows (including the rear window!), cruise control, and full instrumentation were all standard equipment.

The interior is well laid-out in typical Honda fashion, and definitely sporty. The controls are all within easy reach, and all instruments are easily read through the steering wheel. The sports seats are comfortable and supportive, and visibility is excellent. You'll appreciate neat touches like having the cruise control buttons on the steering wheel, a neat little faceplate that folds down to hide the audio system, and several lockable interior storage binnacles.

On the road, the del Sol VTEC doesn't exhibit quite the feeling of lightness that the CRX does—but it's a lot more powerful. Revving this engine to its 8,200-rpm redline is very satisfying, and the VTEC's mid-seven-second 0–60 times put it well ahead of its predecessor (and many other cars as well). There's still a bit of chassis flex, so it's not the ultimate handler some might hope for—but for many that's a fair trade-off for the addition of the open-air driving style. Still, it sticks well enough, with a ride that's more than compliant enough for everyday duty. No complaints with the brake system, which on the VTEC includes vented front disc rotors.

Inside, the del Sol shares much of its hardware with various Civic, Accord, and Prelude models, though the dash was a bit more curvaceously shaped. Dual air bags were standard on this 1994 model. *Honda*

Wheel designs were changed for 1995, as seen on this del Sol Si. Its base model VTEC engine put out less horsepower than the 160-horsepower high-output VTEC model's did, due to its less sophisticated, less costly VTEC system operating only on the intake cams, rather than on both the intake and exhaust side. *Honda*

As noted, the primary changes for 1994 were the addition of the VTEC model and a passenger-side air bag. 1995s received a few more tweaks, with all models getting a low-fuel warning light, a lockable remote trunk release, and a control for the driver-side air vent. Si models got new wheels, larger tires, and the front anti-roll bar from the VTEC. The biggest news for 1995 was the introduction of standard ABS brakes on the VTEC model. A slight reconfiguring of the engine management system and new model numbers for the engines came in 1996, though all basic specs and power output remained the same. The del Sol would finish out its production run virtually unchanged after the 1997 model year.

Hondas are typically well-built, trouble-free cars, and the del Sol is no exception. A review of the car's recall and tech service bulletin history reveals few mechanical issues, though there were minor recalls and service updates relating to various electrical systems. Oil changes are important in any car, but especially one with an 8,200-rpm redline, so a history of frequent engine oil and filter changes is important. A major service to replace the camshaft timing belt and water pump every 90,000 miles is critical (it's worth having it checked at 60K), though the sophisticated VTEC cam timing system has proven remarkably trouble-free. This is an expensive engine to replace—at least 50 percent more than a non-VTEC, SOHC Honda four—so making sure it's in good shape is paramount.

We've heard a few complaints of leaky tops, but that's a function of how often the top is removed, if it's properly stored, and how much sun the seals are exposed to that determines how long they'll last. Fortunately, the top seals are replaceable (though not inexpensive), and the top has proven to be tight and leak-free if in good condition. 1995–1997 models had an updated seal that worked better than the 1993–1994 cars.

Honda enthusiasts are somewhat polarized on the del Sol; some feel it was an improper departure from the tone set by the light, inexpensive, close-coupled CRX. Others point out the del's wailing VTEC engine, and the enjoyment added by the removable top. Some like the styling, some don't. Those are personal choices, but if you want a convertible Honda, and can't afford a new S2000 just yet, then the del Sol remains your only modern-day choice. And if you like it, it's a good one.

It takes a sharp eye to spot the difference on this 1997 del Sol VTEC as opposed to pre-1996 models. Look up front: the somewhat controversial fog lights previously seen just above the front bumper are gone. *Honda*

SPECIFICATIONS (1994 DEL SOL VTEC)

Body style. . . . . Two door, two passenger
Drivetrain layout . . . . front engine, front drive
Engine type . . . . DOHC I-4
Displacement, liter/cc. 1.6-liter/1,595
Horsepower, hp @ rpm . . . . SAE net 160 @ 7,600
Torque, ft-lb @ rpm . . . . SAE net 111 @ 7,000
Transmission . . . . 5-speed manual
Wheelbase, in. 93.3
Length, in. 157.3
Width, in. 66.7
Height, in. 49.4
Base curb weight, lb 2,560
Suspension, f/r. . . . . upper/lower control arms/upper/lower control arms
Steering type. . . . . Rack and pinion
Brakes, f/r. . . . . Disc/disc

PERFORMANCE

Acceleration, 0–60 mph . . . . 7.7 sec.
Standing quarter
mile, sec/mph 15.9/90.0
Source. . . . . Road & Track

TYPICAL PARTS/REPAIR PRICES

Major tune-up/service. $500
Air filter 11
Shock absorber 75
Catalytic converter(s) 81
Clutch replacement 820

WEBSITES

clubsol.com
hondaclub.com

Chapter 14

FOR
- Excellent handling (particularly 1997–1999)
- 190/195/200-horse VTEC engine
- Honda quality

AGAINST
- Expensive
- 1992–1996 model's styling not for everyone, inside and out
- Tight rear-seat area

HOT PICKS
1994–1996 Prelude VTEC, 1999 Prelude Type SH

REPORT CARD

Engine . . . . .A
Transmission . . . . .B
Power/Weight Ratio . . . .A-
Handling . . . . .A
Braking . . . . .B+
Ride . . . . .B+
Exterior Styling . . . . . .C+
Interior Styling . . . . . . .B
Interior Function . . . . . .B+
Cargo Capacity . . . . . .B
Everyday Usability . . . . .A-
Reliability . . . . .A-
Fit and Finish . . . . .A
Market Availability . . . . .A-
Resale Value Potential . . .B
Fun Factor . . . . .B+
Bang for Buck . . . . . . .B
Aftermarket Interest . . .A
Club Support . . . . .A

Honda Prelude (1992–1999)

Up until 1992, Honda's Prelude had always been sporty, yet somehow conservative at the same time; it was often referred to as a "budget-priced, Japanese Mercedes SL" (even though it was never offered in convertible form, which of course all SLs are). Nonetheless, that all changed with a complete re-body for 1992 to a look that is, at minimum, daring. The 1992 Prelude is nearly 3 inches wider and nearly 2 inches lower than its predecessor, with high rear bustle, thick C-pillars, and a sharkish nose that you either love or hate. Equipment levels were up over the previous model, and the 1992 could be had in two trim levels: S or Si. The S is the base model, and of no interest to the enthusiast driver. The Si is worthy of more attention, packing a 2.3-liter, DOHC four with 160 horsepower (this is not to be confused with the del Sol's 1.6-liter VTEC engine that garners the same horsepower rating but has a much different power curve, and was designed for the smaller car). The real enthusiast's Prelude showed up for 1993, packing a VTEC of its own: this one at 2.2-liters, and delivering an amazing 190 horsepower—more than many V-6s and turbo fours of the day, or now.

The 1992 and later Prelude Si is a nice enough piece, and its 160-horse four is nothing to sneeze at. But this is a good-sized car, and its chassis makes you want more. The answer came in 1993 . *Honda*

The answer to the question of chassis strength was called the Prelude VTEC. The VTEC version of the Prelude's 2.2-liter four was good for 30 more horsepower, for a total of 190. The only way to tell the difference from the outside is by the subtle deck-mounted rear wing (or the VTEC badge, of course). *Honda*

Curiously, Honda developed an electronically managed four-wheeled-steering system (called 4WS) that was designed to increase the car's handling ability and reduce the tendency toward understeer—yet it was never offered on the highest performing model. It was later dropped, apparently not worth the cost and potential future upkeep.

As the Prelude VTEC is the top model in the lineup, equipment levels are high, and so is the price:

independent double-wishbone suspension, dual air bags, AC, cruise control, power windows/doors/locks/mirrors/sunroof, a seven-speaker sound system, five-speed manual transmission (no automatic was offered), four-wheel disc brakes with ABS—the list goes on. Add what few options were available, and it wasn't hard to push a fully loaded Prelude VTEC over $25,000—and that was in 1993. But it certainly delivered high content for money.

The Prelude's seating was as good as anything offered in lower line Porsches, though the readability and design of the dash were definitely not. A low dash emphasized an open, "airy" feel, with some switches being mounted on its horizontal surfaces. *Honda*

From an exterior appearance standpoint, things were pretty much status quo from the VTEC's introduction in 1993 through this platform's final year, 1996, as shown. Even the wheels remained the same. This car's look is another one of those "love it or hate it" designs; it's certainly bold, but the front and rear aspects didn't please everyone. *Honda*

The interior is a bit of a paradox: it's well finished in typical Honda fashion, and the seats are excellent. But the rear seats are very cramped, even for kids, and the thick C-pillar creates a blind spot. Honda's interior stylists created a broad sweeping dash design that was supposed to emphasize the airiness of the cabin—as with the exterior look, some like it, and some don't. The dash looks hard and plasticky, the main gauges are smaller than they need to be for design's sake, and the ancillary gauges are offset far to the right, again to fit into the narrow slit meant for them. Funky, but not a great design.

Nobody will complain about the VTEC powerplant, however. *Road & Track,* in a 1994 road test, said, "No doubt, this engine is a linebacker, but one who knows the proper fork to use when the salad is served." Twin balance shafts manage the second order vibrations common to large inline fours, and the VTEC variable valve timing system kicks the engine into its more aggressive cam mode at around 4,800 rpm. From there, it's a steady and sonorous pull up to its 7,400-rpm redline. This fourth-generation Prelude VTEC is a reasonable handler too, though at .84g on the skid pad, it doesn't stick quite as well as some of today's best.

Honda actually mixed the look of several previous-generation Preludes into the new-for-1997 car. The look is clean and modern, and the handling is among the best offered to date by a front-wheel drive car. *Honda*

The current Prelude is less "fastback-ish," and nicely proportioned. All Preludes from 1997 on are VTEC models, and while the Active Torque Transfer System–equipped SH models are exceptional handlers, don't pass up a clean, well-priced standard model—the difference is minimal. *Honda*

Relatively few changes came in 1994: a juggling of equipment levels on S, Si, and 4WS, plus a standard—and nicely executed—leather interior on the 4WS and VTEC Preludes, plus a new map light. The 1995 Prelude VTEC was carried over virtually unchanged, and the 4WS variant was finally dropped. 1996, the final year for this body style, was also largely unchanged.

Five years is usually about all most Japanese carmakers will let one model platform go without an overhaul, so the Prelude was due a makeover for 1997. For this fifth-generation car, Honda reverted to a notchback style not all that unlike the second- and third-gen models, though the hideaway headlights of those models was supplanted by a more modern, faired-in glass arrangement. The Prelude grew a bit over the 1992–1996 car too: 1.3 inches in the wheelbase, 3.2 inches in length, and an inch in height. Most of the benefit went to the rear passenger area, which is now a much more usable place for real people. The suspension hardware—already plenty fine—was largely carried over, though the new chassis was some 50 percent stiffer from a structural standpoint.

Honda also took this opportunity to take the Prelude upmarket a bit: the previous base S and mid-line Si models went away, and all post-1997 Preludes carry the VTEC engine, now revised and re-rated at 195 horsepower. The VTEC cams now cut into high lift mode at 5,000 rpm, and the redline was extended to 7,500 revs. Those 16-inch wheels became standard, and most everything available on fully loaded, previous-generation Preludes was standard as well. A sequentially managed four-speed, automatic transmission was finally added to the option list. The avant-garde dash and interior styling of the previous car was replaced with a downright traditional layout that places all the gauges in a binnacle directly in front of the driver, easily seen through the steering wheel.

If S, Si, and 4WS are gone, what's left? Two variations of VTEC-powered Prelude: the standard car and the new-for-1997 SH. The SH combines yet another innovative system that attempts to make a front-wheel drive car handle more like a rear-wheel drive car. The Active Torque Transfer System (ATTS) consists of two small clutches and a miniature planetary gearbox.

Last of the decade, the 1999 Prelude SH. For some reason, sales never met Honda's expectations, but the Prelude's handling won't disappoint anyone. *Honda*

When cornering, the clutch controlling the outside wheels is hydraulically engaged under computer control. The system can allow one wheel to spin up to 15 percent faster than the other, the byproduct being crisper turn in and less understeer. We don't have space to fully explain the tech, but it works. That said, even the standard car is a remarkable handler, having won an all-out, seven-car sport coupe comparison performed by *Car and Driver* for its December 1999 issue. If the car you want is an SH model, there's no reason to avoid it; yet, don't pass up a non-SH model, as in everyday driving, there's little functional difference in its handling.

As the 1997 was virtually a new car, there were no changes for 1998. Horsepower was increased to an even 200 for 1999 models (195 for automatic-equipped cars), and the VTEC's service interval for a major tune-up was extended to 100,000 miles. 1999 cars also benefited from a keyless entry system, an interior air filter, a new mesh-style front grille, and revised interior fabric and color choices. Based on the superb handling and highest-ever (for a Prelude) power output, it's hard to argue with the latest 1999 models being considered the best of the breed to date.

Preludes tend to be as reliable as any Honda but need their care like any other car. A major service to replace the cam timing belts is required at 60,000 miles, and this is a good time to replace the water pump, accessory belts, and cooling hoses too. The VTEC hardware is an extra element of sophistication, and though its has proven extremely reliable, rebuilding the engine, or at least the head, is a 30–40 percent costlier proposition than it is on cars without the cam trickery. The 1992–1996 Preludes have occasional electronic and engine management system problems, and replacing the special gauges, if they fail, will be expensive. 1997 and later Preludes have proven to have few foibles so far.

The Prelude has never been the ultra-strong seller Honda had hoped for, yet other than the Civic, is the one of its longest-standing nameplates. Some feel that the popularity of the smaller Acura Integra—which costs less but carries an upmarket nameplate—has somewhat capped the Prelude's popularity. But it's a larger, more well-equipped car, and it's hard to argue with its 190–200 horsepower personality. Prices for good used Preludes tend to be attractive, and if you want something slightly larger than most of the compact models, it's worth a look, in either fourth- or fifth-generation form.

SPECIFICATIONS (1997 PRELUDE TYPE SH)

Body style. . . . . Two door, four passenger
Drivetrain layout. . . . . Front engine, front drive
Engine type . . . . DOHC I-4
Displacement, liter/cc. 2.2-liter/2,157
Horsepower, hp @ rpm . . . . SAE net 195 @ 7,000
Torque, ft-lb @ rpm . . . . SAE net 156 @ 5,250
Transmission . . . . 5-speed manual
Wheelbase, in. 101.8
Length, in. 178.0
Width, in. 69.0
Height, in. 51.8
Base curb weight, lb 3,045
Suspension, f/r . . . . Upper and lower control arms/upper and lower control arms
Steering type. . . . . Rack and pinion
Brakes, f/r. . . . . Disc/disc

PERFORMANCE

Acceleration, 0–60 mph . . . . 7.7 sec.
Standing quarter
mile, sec/mph 15.8/89.7
Source. . . . . Road & Track

TYPICAL PARTS/REPAIR PRICES

Major tune-up/service. $500
Air filter 23
Shock absorber 80
Catalytic converter(s) 90
Clutch replacement 800

WEBSITES

hondaprelude.com
superhonda.com
hondaclub.com

Chapter 15

FOR
- A 100 percent pure-top-down sports car
- Great handler, fun to drive
- Rock-solid reliability

AGAINST
- Too small for some
- Cheap top materials
- Choppy freeway ride

HOT PIC
1997 STO "M Edition," 1999 10th Anniversary M Edition

REPORT CARD

Engine	B
Transmission	A
Power/Weight Ratio	B
Handling	A
Braking	B
Ride	B
Exterior Styling	A
Interior Styling	A
Interior Function	B
Cargo Capacity	B-
Everyday Usability	B
Reliability	A-
Fit and Finish	A-
Market Availability	A
Resale Value Potential	B
Fun Factor	A
Bang for Buck	A
Aftermarket Interest	A
Club Support	A

Mazda Miata (1990–1999)

If the notion of a sports car means a compact rear drive, modestly priced, two-seat convertible to you, then the Mazda Miata is the quintessential sports car. Not a powerful, technical tour de force like its big brother the RX-7, or a broad-shouldered V-8 power musclecar like a Corvette, the Miata is an elemental sports car that's really quite British in concept, if Japanese in execution. And it's interesting to note that while the Miata is clearly inspired by legions of English roadsters, such as the MGB, Sunbeam Alpine, Triumph TR4, and Lotus Elan, it has outsold all of them put together, many times over. In fact, with over a half-million sold in less than a decade, it's already one of the best-selling sports cars of all time.

As with Mustangs and certain other cars, Miata owners continually debate whether the earliest 1.6-liter cars, the later 1.8-liter models, or the second-generation 1999 and later Miatas are really the best expression of Mazda's best selling sports car. It doesn't matter; they're all fun to drive. This is a 1992 model. *Mazda*

Top up or down, these 1992 Miatas represent pure, elemental sports car styling with a shape that is sure to wear well for a long time. The M Edition in the foreground wears genuine BBS alloy wheels. *Mazda*

Disclaimer: There's too much material, and too many model variations, for us to cover in one chapter. You might say the Miata deserves its own book—and indeed there are several, not to mention devout owners' clubs and many specialist parts and service providers. We can only give you the basics, so if you ultimately determine that you are interested in a Miata, we suggest you browse your bookstore, the Web, and talk to the clubbies to get more information on the model and spec that will best suit your needs.

The Miata—officially called the MX-5 Miata and launched in late 1989 as a 1990 model—is certainly equipped with the right sports car DNA. It has a two-seats-only, convertible body style; lightweight; a fully independent suspension; power four-wheel disc brakes; quick and communicative rack-and-pinion steering; a

The 1994 M Edition. The small glass lenses in the upper front fascia area not only house the turn signal and parking lights, but also allow the driver to "flash" the high beams at another vehicle without fully raising the pop-up lights. *Mazda*

This 1993 Limited Edition sports not only BBS wheels but the first signs of the R model sport versions to follow. It has a slightly beefier suspension and a small chin spoiler that mimics the look of the one on the Mazda RX-7 R1. *Mazda*

willing—if not overly powerful—DOHC four-cylinder engine powering the rear wheels; and a driver-side air bag. A five-speed manual is standard, and is highly recommended over the optional four-speed automatic. The trunk holds a weekend's worth of luggage, and the AC, heater, and stereo are all up to top-down duty. What might loosely be called the Series I Miatas (our term only, not an official Mazda designation) were powered by a 1.6-liter four rated at 116 horsepower. There was a base model and two option packages: the A package added a leather-wrapped steering wheel, alloy wheels, power steering, and an upgraded sound system. The B package further added power windows, cruise control, and nifty headrest-mounted stereo speakers. AC was an option on all models, as was a limited-slip differential, the aforementioned automatic, and a removable

Even though the Miata had already received numerous detail improvements and a displacement increase by the time of this 1995 model, its outward appearance, in standard form, had changed little. This original body style would carry the car from 1990 through the 1997 model year. *Mazda*

hard top. While this item certainly makes the Miata quieter, cozier, and more secure, it's a pain to remove and store, and takes away the spontaneity of dropping the top. Something to consider if you live in cold, rainy climes.

Few changes occurred from the initial 1990 models through 1993, but the car got a substantive update for 1994. The "Series 2" Miata's most notable improvement was a new 1.8-liter engine; the increased displacement was good for an increase in horsepower from 116 to 128 (then later 133), plus a 10 ft-lb

Here's an interesting twist on the Miata theme, a Mazda-designed concept car called the Miata Coupe. All production Miatas are convertibles, but with this car the company explored the notion of building a closed coupe version. Not surprisingly, the Miata Coupe resembles its larger brother, the RX-7. Mazda ultimately decided that a drop top was part of the car's appeal, and elected not to build the Miata Coupe, but it's an attractive proposition nonetheless. *Mazda*

increase in torque. *Road & Track's* test numbers evidenced a drop in 0–60 times from 9.5 seconds for the 1.6-liter version to 8.7 for the larger-engined car—not earth shattering, but enough to feel. Additional revisions included some chassis-stiffening measures to reduce "cowl shake" (a condition to which many unibody-chassised convertibles are prone); a larger gas tank; increased brake rotor diameter for increased resistance to brake fade; an uprated Torsen rear differential; and a standard passenger-side air bag. All in all, a better Miata.

For 1995, the A and B option packages were combined into one "Popular Equipment" option, and leather upholstery was added to the option list. Engine management and intake systems revisions raised the 1.8's horsepower to an even 140 for 1996, though most enthusiast magazine test numbers were virtually identical. The revisions that encompass these Series 2 models essentially carried the Miata through 1996, 1997, and early 1998, but there were several special models along the way. One was the R model, which was designed to deliver maximum handling prowess to those who really

The 1996 M Edition (see sidebar). *Mazda*

M AND SPECIAL EDITION MIATAS

Miata M Edition STO. *Mazda*

As noted, Mazda has conjured up a special (most often referred to as M Edition) Miata just about every year since inception. Some have been little more than paint and upholstery combinations that weren't offered on the standard model, while others have included notable hardware revisions or upgrades. Most are generally more collectible to the Miataphile than standard production cars; though depending on your enthusiast interest, they may or may not be worth seeking out or worth paying any more for. Here's a brief look at those that have appeared during our 1990–1999 time frame:

1991 BRG Edition—British Racing Green paint, tan top, and tan leather interior. Special because it's a very traditional sports car look, and represents the start of the M Edition lineup.

1992 Black Edition—Black paint, tan top, 14-inch BBS wheels. A nice looker, but otherwise nothing special.

1992 Yellow Edition—Little more than triple-coat sunburst yellow paint, though this remains among the rarest M Edition Miatas sold: just 1,519 copies.

1993 Limited Edition—Much like the Black Edition car, with an upgraded suspension, BBS wheels, and a snappy-looking red tonneau cover. Also rare at just 1,505 copies.

1994 M Edition—Montego Blue Mica paint, tan top, and leather interior. Nardi wood-trimmed steering wheel and e-brake handle—even a special key ring and lapel pin.

1995 M Edition—Much the same as the 1994, finished in a deep red (Merlot Mica) paint scheme and now sporting 15-inch BBS wheels.

1996 M.5 Edition—This time it was Starlight Blue Mica paint, 15-inch Enkei sport wheels, upgraded audio system.

1997 M Edition—Marina Green Mica paint, polished six-spoke wheels, and more M-owner trinkets.

1997.5 STO—A leather-upholstered R model in Twilight Blue Mica paint with a tan interior and top. Some equipment differences as compared to pure R model; STO stands for Special Touring Option.

1999 10th Anniversary—3,000 built for U.S. consumption, and the first M Edition to appear on the new platform. Sapphire Blue Mica paint with coordinated blue top and boot, black/blue interior package with Nardi wheel, chrome 16-inch wheels, sport suspension and body kit. First availability of six-speed manual transmission. If you buy one, make sure to get the special "owner kit" consisting of a diecast model, key chain, and his/hers 10th Anniversary Miata Seiko watches.

Source: *Collectible Automobile*

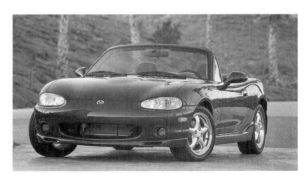

Miata 10th Anniversary Edition.

Other than 14-inch wheels, there's not a lot that separates the appearance of this 1997 Miata from an original 1990 model. *Mazda*

like to carve canyons on the weekend and/or participate in weekend club racing events. The R, which showed up in mid-1994 and was sold through 1996, features a firmer suspension, special alloy wheels, a standard limited-slip differential, and front/rear spoilers. These are quite popular with the club types, and usually command substantial premiums; also be careful about buying one that's had too many racing miles on it. Mazda's product planners have also had a great time coming up with several Miata M or SE Editions over the years, each of which combines a special color scheme and equipment mix (see sidebar).

Miata sales remained consistently strong, yet after nearly nine years on the market, it was time for something new. The challenge was formidable: how to freshen the Miata enough to make it new, without diluting its core values, and chasing away the enthusiasm earned by the original.

The new-for-1999 Miata featured a revised chassis that was torsionally stiffer than that of the 1994 models; cowl shake was virtually eliminated this time, and a stiffer chassis also allows for more precise handling. The wheelbase remained the same and the original styling themes were retained, though the body panels were, in actuality, all new. The biggest physical change was the use of faired-in glass headlamp clusters in place of the previous, pop-up units. The interior was upgraded with higher quality materials, and the convertible top got a heated glass rear window in place of the previous unit's plastic backlight. The 1.8-liter engine remained the same, though many mechanical refinements went into the new car. For the first time, a close-ratio six-speed manual transmission showed up on the 1999 model's 10th Anniversary edition car. Naturally, standard equipment, option packages, and color combinations were all reshuffled.

The all-new, just-about-from-the-ground-up 1999 Miata actually bowed in early 1998. The car looks larger, more substantial, and even more curvaceous than the original, though it's not necessarily better looking. The biggest change up front is the replacement of the hideaway headlights with flush glass units. The 15-inch wheels are now standard. *Long Shot Photography*

The 10th Anniversary Edition has just about every goody Mazda could fit on and in it, including the sport package's 16-inch wheels, front spoiler, and special rocker panels.

We've driven and tested many a Miata, and generally (and personally) speaking, the newer they are, the better they are. We prefer the 1999 and newer cars, though they are still somewhat newish as of this writing; going back from there, we'd have to say the 1996–1998 Miatas with the 140-horse motors are the best of the early body style cars. Then, we'd recommend a 1994–1995 model, and finally the 1.6-liter Miatas if that's all your budget allows. That said, they are all a ton of fun to drive. The engine is adequate if not awe inspiring, and not overwhelmingly smooth, but it loves to rev, and sounds great for a small four. The five-speed "snicks" satisfyingly from gear to gear, there's very little body roll, and the Miata serves up plenty of road/steering/brake feel.

The Miata has proven to be a tough, reliable car, right from the earliest models. Naturally, we suggest the newest, lowest-mileage car you can afford, but don't shy away from a really well-cared-for example with up to 100,000 miles on it. Timing belts need to be replaced every 60,000 miles, so look for receipts for this repair. When changing the belt, it's good to address any other items that can be easily accessed while the front end of the engine is torn down, such as a worn water pump, cam belt tensioner, crankshaft seal, and accessory belts. According to *Miata Magazine*, the crankshafts on 1990 and early 1991 models are prone to breakage. Batteries are a weak point; the Miata uses a special size and type of battery that's mounted in the trunk, and they tend to just die without warning. Unless the car you buy has a fresh battery in it, change it before you are stranded.

Spark plug wires, especially on 1.6-liter cars, don't usually go past about 40,000 miles or so. Shock absorbers also tend to be short lived (though easily replaced). Bad shocks will cause a rough ride, vibration, and premature tire wear, so like the battery, change them if you can't prove how old, or new, they

The later interior is a bit roomier and a little more up to date than that of the 1990–1997 Miatas, though it still exhibits the same intelligent packaging of the original. The dash incorporates hardware previously unheard of on sports cars, such as dual air bags and a CD player.

are. Clutches tend to last, but not the clutch slave cylinder—leakage is common in earlier cars, but replacement is easy and inexpensive. Exhaust systems can last 100,000 miles, or as little as 60,000, depending on how the car is driven.

Interior materials and fabrics are not of super quality and tend to wear if the car is consistently parked outside with the top down; the use of a good vinyl protectant and a car cover go a long way here. And the top itself is no paragon of quality either: it goes up and down easily and seals well, but the materials wear out quickly, and the plastic rear window on pre-1999 cars turns to yellow haze—then hardens and tears out of the top. Fortunately, the aftermarket makes tops of higher quality, some with glass windows, and these are worth installing.

It's simple: If you want a real sports car that's a ball to drive, remarkably reliable, affordable to buy and own, and don't mind its pint size, it is awfully hard to beat a Miata.

The early Miata cabin is straightforward and attractive, though the large air bag steering wheel looks a bit clunky compared to more modern versions. Keep the top up and the car covered, or these interiors tend to pay the price. *Mazda*

SPECIFICATIONS (1996 MIATA)

Body style . . . . Two door, two passenger
Drivetrain layout . . . . Front engine, rear drive
Engine type . . . . DOHC I-4
Displacement, liter/cc 1.8/1,839
Horsepower, hp @ rpm . . . . SAE net 133 @ 6,500
Torque, ft-lb @ rpm . . . . SAE net 114 @ 5,500
Transmission . . . . 5-speed manual
Wheelbase, in. 89.2
Length, in. 155.4
Width, in. 65.9
Height, in. 48.2
Base curb weight, lb 2,293
Suspension, f/r . . . . Upper and lower A-arms/upper and lower A-arms
Steering type. . . . . Rack and pinion
Brakes, f/r . . . . Disc/disc

PERFORMANCE

Acceleration, 0-60 mph . . . . 8.8 sec.
Standing quarter
mile, sec/mph 16.6/83.0
Source . . . . Road & Track

TYPICAL PARTS/REPAIR PRICES

Major tune-up/service. $400
Air filter 12
Shock absorber 70
Catalytic converter(s) 82
Clutch replacement 495

WEBSITES

miata.net

Mazda RX-7 (1993–1996)

REPORT CARD

Engine	A+
Transmission	A
Power/Weight Ratio	A
Handling	A+
Braking	A
Ride	B
Exterior Styling	A
Interior Styling	A
Interior Function	B
Cargo Capacity	B
Everyday Usability	B-
Reliability	B
Fit and Finish	B+
Market Availability	C
Resale Value Potential	A-
Fun Factor	A+
Bang for Buck	A
Aftermarket Interest	A
Club Support	A

There are "sports cars," and then there are *sports cars*. As mentioned, when trying to decide what marques and models to include in this book, we definitely broadened the definition of a sports car a bit, so as to add in several nice-driving machines that dish up some modicum of fun, yet can serve as affordable, everyday transport. The third-generation Mazda RX-7 needs no such definitional assistance. It is a pure, unadulterated sports car, perhaps among the most ardent of sports cars in this book.

The original RX-7 of 1979 was too, yet somehow over the years, it got watered down. The second-generation RX was a nice enough car but a bit soft in the middle. Enthusiasts screamed for something tauter and with higher performance—they got both with the new car introduced in mid-1992 as a 1993 model.

The third-gen RX-7 was all new from the ground up, and the primary design focus was on lightweight with minimum gadgetry. The

Mazda's new-for-1993 RX-7 was as new as new could get. Its design premises included light weight and a structurally stiff chassis to maximize performance and handling. This is a Touring model. *Mazda*

The RX-7's designers purposefully kept the passenger compartment somewhat inboard of the fenderline to give the car "shoulders" and a more substantially grounded appearance. Jaguar also used this to great effect with the legendary—and still beautiful—E-Type of the 1960s and early 1970s. *Mazda*

chassis is an ultra-torsionally stiff monocoque, offered only in two-seat coupe form. It's just large enough to hold its mechanicals, two people, and a weekend's luggage. The curvaceous skin, replete with Italian Zagato-inspired double roof bubbles, is stretched so tight that it fairly pings when you touch it. The RX-7 employs a traditional double-wishbone suspension front and rear, featuring lightweight alloy control arms and anti-roll bars. The rear end contains a Torsen limited-slip differential, and the brakes are as you'd expect: Four-wheel vented discs with standard ABS. Steering is via a power-assisted, speed-sensitive rack and pinion, with a cat-quick 15.0:1 ratio.

The good news is under the hood, in the form of Mazda's first-ever-for-the-street, twin-turbo rotary engine. The twin-turbos are staged to add boost sequentially, preserving a measure of low-end torque, combined with adequate volume to make big horsepower at maximum boost (the Toyota Supra's system operates much the same way). Power is improved, and detonation risk reduced, via an air-to-air intercooler,

and the RX could be ordered with your choice of a five-speed manual transmission or a four-speed automatic (we heartily recommend the former!).

Although its 255 horsepower and 217 ft-lb of torque rating may not sound like much compared to those in the 300 horsepower club, remember that performance is a function of both power and weight—and the RX-7's fighting weight is a mere 2,800 pounds. Contrast that to a fully loaded Mitsubishi 3000GT VR-4, which tilts the scales at over 1,000 pounds more.

Inside, the RX is all business: an enveloping cockpit that puts the driver first, with all gauges and controls falling readily to hand. Air conditioning, power steering/windows/mirrors/locks, and a decent sound system are all standard. Visibility over the curvaceous front fenders is excellent, though the thickish B-pillar might create a blind spot for some drivers. The cabin is tight, though encapsulating in almost a race car sort of way. There were few options: the Touring option group (leather upholstery, a power sunroof, and an

Although the somewhat flat rear deck might give you the impression that the RX-7 has a conventional trunk, it is indeed a hatchback. The rear taillight design resembles that of the Camaro Z28, which was also new in 1993. *Mazda*

upgraded Bose sound system) and the R1 handling package (further upgraded shocks, twin oil coolers, black rubber front spoiler, rear wing, and Z-rated tires). This handling option was renamed R-2 for model years 1993 and 1994.

Driving it is clearly the best part. *Motor Trend* describes the experience in its "1993 Import Car of the Year" article, an award which the RX-7 handily won: "The only cars that get around Sear Point International Raceway's hill loop much faster have numbers on the doors. No street car shy of almost double the price—and few far beyond that—can touch the sequentially twin-turbocharged Mazda RX-7 on such a sinuous circuit. . . . It's within one foot of being the shortest-stopping street car we've ever tested; out-accelerates anything that doesn't have a third more horsepower (and many that do); reaches 160 miles per hour in less than three miles; and grips the road harder than the best race cars of only a few years ago."

It's fun to feel the turbos do their sequential boost thing: power starts off modestly at very low rpm, then the first, smaller turbo cuts in with a surge; then a slight "dent" in the power delivery as soon as the second (larger) blower is phased in. The shift throws are short, body roll is about nil, the steering is quick and communicative, and the brakes are beyond impressive. Rotary engines are known for their smoothness, and the RX's spins happily to its 8,000-rpm redline—and to a 0–60 time of around 5.0-seconds; a "driver's car" if there ever was.

Give careful thought to the R1 suspension option if you are looking at a 1993 model; while it does maximize the RX-7's handling capability, the cost is a nearly punishing ride on all but the smoothest of surfaces. If max cornering ability is your thing, and/or you plan to use the car for an occasional weekend slalom or club race, it's great. If not, and the RX will be your everyday ride, we'd recommend a non-R1-equipped

The easiest ways to spot an R1- or R2-equipped RX-7 is by the hard plastic lower front spoiler and the body-colored rear deck wing. The original R1 package was just a bit much for the street but great on the track. The package was softened and renamed R2 for 1994, and further re-calibrated for 1995; either of the latter two present a nice street ride/performance handling balance. *David Newhardt*

car. The package was renamed R2 for 1994, which included slightly softer shock settings and a switch to Pirelli tires; shock tuning was further tamed for 1995, putting it very near that of the 1993 Touring spec, and making it a much more palpable balance between max handling prowess and daily livability.

There were few changes throughout the third-gen RX-7's short production life. Many were running mechanical updates; 1994–1995 models generally have more robust interior and exterior finishes, plus the above-noted changes to the uprated suspension option. And there were some recalls, so it's best to check and see if your subject car has been given the requisite updates.

The biggest maintenance issue with an RX is the care and feeding of its twin-turbo, twin-rotor engine. You've already heard us tell you about how regular engine oil and filter changes are important with reference to several other cars in this book; with the RX-7, this regimen is critical. Although these later series

The RX-7's engine is like no other anywhere. Besides being, by that time, Mazda's only use of the Wankel rotary engine in the United States, the 1993–1995 represented the only twin-turbocharged version ever offered in the marketplace. *Mazda*

rotaries don't burn seals and guzzle oil like those of the 1970s, they still like clean, fresh lubricant with a minimum of contaminants. Cooling systems also need to be drained and refilled per the owners manual.

The turbos are not interchangeable, and though their bearings and other innards are reasonably tough, they could need rebuilding by as soon as 75,000 miles. They will definitely need attention by 100,000, unless given superb care. Transmissions are reasonably sturdy, though second-gear synchros will go first. The clutch's

Mazda put the RX-7's tach right where it belongs—square in front of the driver, because the twin-turbo rotary will quickly and easily rev to redline. The balance of the controls are easy to reach, and like the rest of the car, oriented toward the driver. Note short, quick-actioned shifter. *Mazda*

life will be determined by how hard the car was driven, though the rear Torsen diff should last forever.

A few minor electrical gremlins show up in these cars, certainly uncharacteristic for a modern-day Japanese product but not enough to keep you from buying one. The "Engine" warning light will often appear for no reason, only to later shut itself off. Generally speaking, the later the car, the fewer of these issues are likely to crop up. The biggest one to watch is the temperature gauge, as its reading is not at all linear in relation to actual engine temp. In other words, the needle doesn't tend to move off the "normal" range of the gauge until the engine is really running hot and not too far from overheating. All the RX-7 clubs can clue you in as to the fix, but make sure the car you are looking at hasn't been overheated—an expensive proposition for sure.

It's a shame that the enthusiast market didn't better embrace the car it asked for; the RX went away after only three model years, though it was offered in Japan for several more. According to a website put up by Mazda employee Mike Haun, fewer than 14,000 third-generation RX-7s were imported for U.S. consumption. By 1995—the last official model year the RX-7 model was sold here, though supply lasted well into 1996—a fully loaded R-2 model was a near $40,000 ride, which started to seem like an expensive proposition at the time. But in relation to Boxsters and Z3s which now easily cost that much (or a lot more), the RX-7 really wasn't overly expensive. Fine examples still bring strong prices, and deliver a single-minded, high-performance driving experience that's hard to match.

SPECIFICATIONS (1993 RX-7 TOURING)

Body style . . . . Two door, two passenger
Drivetrain layout . . . . Front engine, rear drive
Engine type . . . . Twin rotor Wankel
Displacement, liter/cc . . . . Twin-turbo 1.3/1,308
Horsepower, hp @ rpm . . . . SAE net 255 @ 6,500
Torque, ft-lb @ rpm . . . . SAE net 217 @ 5,000
Transmission . . . . 5-speed manual
Wheelbase, in. 96.5
Length, in. 168.5
Width, in. 68.9
Height, in. 48.4
Base curb weight, lb 2,862
Suspension, f/r. . . . . Upper and lower A-arms/multilink
Steering type. . . . . Rack and pinion
Brakes, f/r. . . . . Disc/disc

PERFORMANCE

Acceleration, 0–60 mph . . . . 4.9 sec.
Standing quarter
mile, sec/mph 13.5
Source. . . . . Road & Track

TYPICAL PARTS/REPAIR PRICES

Major tune-up/service. $425
Air filter 13
Shock absorber 99
Catalytic converter(s) 88
Clutch replacement 700

WEBSITES

nav.webring.yahoo.com/hub?ring=rx7clubsonly&list

Chapter 17

Mitsubishi 3000GT VR-4/Dodge Stealth R/T Turbo (1991–1999/1991–1996)

FOR
- Aggressive styling
- 300+ horsepower
- High-tech driveline

AGAINST
- Expensive to maintain
- Rear seat almost useless
- Too gimmicky for some

HOT PICK
1995–1996 3000GT VR-4

REPORT CARD

Engine	A-
Transmission	A-
Power/Weight Ratio	B-
Handling	B
Braking	B
Ride	B+
Exterior Styling	A-
Interior Styling	B+
Interior Function	B
Cargo Capacity	B
Everyday Usability	B
Reliability	B
Fit and Finish	B+
Market Availability	B-
Resale Value Potential	B
Fun Factor	B+
Bang for Buck	B
Aftermarket Interest	B+
Club Support	B

You have to credit Mitsubishi for coming to market with a car like the 3000GT. Here was a company, known primarily (in the United States) for building decent economy sedans and semi-sporty coupes. Then in 1991, it rolls out a curvaceously styled, technology packed, all-wheel-drive semi-exotic that had as much horsepower as the current-day Ferrari. And the 3000 certainly had legs, for it ran from 1991 through 1999 in much the same form. Much the same can be said for the Dodge Stealth, a slightly re-skinned version of the same underpinnings, styled and marketed by Dodge from 1991 through the 1996 model year. Although both were available in several naturally aspirated forms over

Ferrari or Mitsubishi? The 1991 3000GT lineup certainly did crib a bit of its look from the Ferrari 308-328 models. Note blisters atop the hood, which were a last-minute add-on once it was determined that the hood didn't clear the top of the shock towers. *Mitsubishi*

Mitsu must have also been looking at another Ferrari model, the midengined Testarossa, as it surely inspired the 3000GT VR-4's straked side scoops. Even if the detailing is a bit fussy, the overall shape is pleasing. *Mitsubishi*

From the back you can see two of the features that appeal to those who really enjoy technotoys: the rear wing (one element of the Active Aero system) could be raised and lowered. Although the mufflers look like those of a stock exhaust system, a switch in the passenger compartment allowed the selection of a quieter mode, perhaps for sneaking home late at night. We suspect most owners set the system to the louder setting and leave it there. *Mitsubishi*

Although the VR-4 was getting on in years by 1997, Mitsubishi continued to update and freshen the car to keep it in the game. This 1997 demonstrates the new 18-inch wheel design, slightly revised front fascia, new fog lights, and an all-new rear wing, sans the Active Aero feature. To most eyes, these are the handsomest VR-4s yet. *Mitsubishi*

The VR-4 even got a mild facelift for its final year, 1999, which leads us to believe Mitsu had considered keeping it around longer and then ultimately thought better of it; perhaps not to steal any thunder from the new-for-2000, V-6-powered Eclipse that was on the way. The front fascia was again redesigned, this time with a simple, though aggressive, open nose. *Mitsubishi*

And along came a Spyder: this photo shows not only the rare, and expensive, retractable hardtop Spyder VR-4 version, but the restyle that came along for 1995. New exposed headlights were supposedly styled after a mythical Japanese warrior's mask; no matter, most viewed the look as an improvement. Front fascia and side scoops were also cleaned up in the process. *Mitsubishi*

The other big change for 1999, and we do mean big, was an all-new rear wing that for the first time did not in any way inhibit rear visibility. While it looks like an aftermarket piece, it was in fact installed by the factory and was probably a better solution than the Active Aero system from the beginning. *Mitsubishi*

the years, the top performance model is the twin-turbocharged 3000GT VR-4, with the Dodge version called the Stealth R/T Turbo; these are the cars we'll concentrate on here, and reference them both by the Mitsubishi version. Also, there were so many small changes over nearly a decade, and the platform was sold in so many versions, it's impossible to address every update and modification in this small space, so we suggest you get involved with the various owners' clubs and cruise the many 3000GT/Stealth websites to get more details on the specific model at which you may be looking.

The VR-4 was a technical tour de force when launched in 1991, packing an unbelievable amount of hardware into its sexy 2+2 bodywork: A twin-turbocharged, intercooled 3.0-liter DOHC V-6 rated at an impressive 300 horsepower; a five-speed manual transmission; full-time all-wheel-drive with a 45/55 front/rear power split; four-wheel independent suspension with four-wheel steering, which operates off a pump driven by the rear powertrain assembly; limited-slip rear differential; 17-inch alloy wheels; cockpit adjustable shock absorbers; four-wheel disc brakes with ABS; an "Active Aero system," which adjusts the rear wing and front air dam heights, depending on vehicle speed; and even an "Active Exhaust system," which allows the drive to electrically select a quieter, or louder, exhaust note (yes, Mitsubishi had finally invented the much-joked about "muffler bearing").

The interior is goody-packed as well, including full instrumentation and then some: a compass, turbo boost gauge, a graphic equalizer for the standard 100-watt sound system; and even red, amber, and blue graphics to demonstrate the settings for the HVAC system. As the VR-4 was the top model offering, all the usual power assists are standard, including windows, door locks, mirrors, and seats. Additional standard

features include a driver-side air bag, cruise control, tilt wheel, and an anti-theft system. With all this hardware packed into a rather compact interior, you'd expect the ergonomics to be a little fussy, and they are. Additionally, the low greenhouse creates just-adequate headroom, and the rear seats are vestigial at best. However, many drivers like the cosseting, racy feel of the 3000/Stealth cabin, so that remains a matter of personal choice (and personal size!).

The first-generation 3000GT VR-4 competed handily with cars like the Nissan 300ZX turbo in terms of performance and price, and it won *Motor Trend*'s Import Car of the Year award for 1991. 1992 was a carryover year, as the car was all new from the ground up for 1991. 1993 also saw relatively few

As with the 3000GT's appearance and powertrains, the interior was mildly but consistently upgraded over the years. This 1997 evidences audio controls on the steering wheel, but the main dash design and gauge layout remained much the same, and always looked good. *Mitsubishi*

changes, those being the addition of a standard keyless entry system, the previously optional leather upholstery also becoming standard, and new options in the form of chrome-plated alloy wheels and an automatic CD changer. The VR-4 engine received a tougher crankshaft and main bearing design in the name of greater long-term reliability, though power outputs remained the same.

The VR-4's first big remodel came along for 1994. In Mitsubishi's own words, the exterior was redesigned to "remove clutter" from the look in the form of new flush glass headlights (replacing the previous hideaway lights); a new hood, which incorporates the previously added-on "blisters" that made room for the tall strut towers; revised (and cleaner looking) side scoops; freshened lower front and rear fascias; and new 17-inch wheels. The interior remained much the same, though a passenger-side air bag was added as standard equipment and the sound system was upgraded.

Knowing that a new twin-turbo Toyota Supra was on the way, Mitsubishi also upped the hardware level on the VR-4. The engine was modified slightly to increase performance, now rated at 320 horsepower and 315 ft-lb of torque, and the previous five-speed Getrag manual transmission was swapped for a six-speed from the same maker. Brake rotor size was increased at all four corners, and the rear calipers were changed to a new two-piston design. Although style always remains a matter of personal choice, most feel the redesign was successful, making the 3000GT VR-4 better looking than ever, and its overall performance was incrementally improved as well.

Nineteen ninety-five saw the introduction of an alternate body style in the form of the 3000 GT Spyder, which was available in naturally aspirated and twin-turbo VR-4 form.

The Mitsubishi-engineered-and-built twin-turbo V-6 was always identical whether it found itself in a VR-4 or Dodge Stealth. Even though the intake and intercooler pluming is certainly long, turbo boost lag is commendably minimal. Be warned, however, as with the twin-turbo powerplants found on the 300ZX, RX-7, and Supra, this is not an inexpensive motor to repair or replace if it goes bang, so good care is critical. *Mitsubishi*

Dodge stylists made a reasonable effort to differentiate the Stealth's appearance from that of the 3000GT. Some felt it was actually the nicer looking of the two. Just about every panel is different, as are wheels and lighting treatments. *DaimlerChrysler*

Most unique about the Spyder is its one-touch, power-actuated convertible hard top, which folded itself neatly into the trunk area. There's no soft top, and no need for a removable hard top or tonneau cover—this concept hadn't been employed on a production car since the Ford Skyliner "retractable" of the late 1950s. Spyders were built in very limited quantity by ASC, a specialty conversion firm, and at a very high price; it's not likely you'll find one for less than our $20,000 price limit for some time. The Spyder body style was exclusive to the Mitsubishi line; no Stealth version was offered.

Other changes for 1995 included an optional power sunroof for all coupe models, new 18-inch performance tires and chromed alloy wheels for the VR-4, minor suspension re-tuning to go along with the new rolling stock, and some color changes. Since both 1994 and 1995 represented a lot of new or revised hardware and substantial investment on the part of Mitsubishi, 1996 saw little of either. Interior and exterior color offerings were revised, and a panic feature was added to the keyless entry/security system. Even though the car had been on the market for five model years (an eternity for a Japanese GT), the 3000 lineup demonstrated it had considerable "legs" in the

marketplace, as in 1996 it outsold the Mazda RX-7, Toyota Supra, and final year Nissan 300ZX combined.

A minor freshening of the overall look came in 1997, in terms of a new front fascia with revised fog lights and a new rear spoiler sans the somewhat troublesome Active Aero feature. The audio system was again upgraded, and a new 10-disc CD changer was optional. 1998 brought about few changes in the form of a few new colors and a revised climate-control read-out, and the power sunroof was made standard equipment. Considering that 1999 was to be the 3000 GT's final year, it's amazing Mitsubishi invested a penny in it. Yet, it found some spare change for a new (and really big) rear wing and slightly revised front and rear fascias.

The Dodge Stealth version went through much of the same evolution as did the 3000GT, except that it had a slightly lower content level and price point. For example, the Stealth never had the Active Aero system. For 1995, Dodge removed the four-wheel steering and electronically shock absorbers, again with an eye toward reducing cost. Credit Dodge and Mitsubishi for working relatively hard to make the cars look different; all of the body panels, save the roof, are unique to each model—which you like best is up to you. As noted, the Mitsubishi-platformed Stealth went away after the 1996 model year.

There's little doubt that the VR-4/R/T Turbo is an exciting car to drive. With 0–60 coming up in less than six seconds, a top speed well over 150, and cornering grip measuring around .9g, they are fast cars by any standard. All-wheel-drive cars tend to have a fairly neutral handling attitude (little understeer or oversteer), and the VR-4 is no exception. One thing to be aware of, however, is that when they do lose traction and break loose, they do so quickly, with little warning, and are usually tough to "recover." This doesn't mean that the VR-4 is unsafe; it just means that it's a fast, powerful car that should be driven with care by an experienced driver at high speeds. Visibility isn't great, due to the thick rear pillar, and the wing, which is visible through the rear window. The biggest gripe from a dynamics standpoint is weight—a fully loaded VR-4 with a full tank of gas is a 4,000-pound car.

The rear end received less work-over than did the rest of the car. The five-spoke "blender blade" wheels are clearly on the far side of good taste. *DaimlerChrysler*

Compare that with the relatively lithe Mazda RX-7, which weighs something like 1,200 pounds less, and accomplishes at least equal performance, in spite of its 45-65 horsepower deficit. Throw the VR-4 hard into a corner, and you can feel all that inertia working against the tires and suspension. Still, it's a nice-handling, fast GT.

As you've gathered by now, these are complicated cars, with many systems. As these systems (awd, 4ws, Active Aero and Exhaust, electronic shocks, and two turbos) wear out and need repair or replacement, the VR-4 can become a very expensive car to keep on the road, though they are basically reliable by nature. A major engine service is required every 60,000 miles that includes the replacement of the cam belt, accessory belts, the water pump, and several filters plus many adjustments; this service must be done regularly to avoid problems down the line. By now, you're tired of us harping about consistent and frequent oil changes, but they are critical when it comes to a twin-turbocharged engine.

Most of the electrical accessories have proven relatively reliable, with the exception of the rear wing on the Active Aero system, the motor for which often fails. Due to their weight and and propensity for hard

driving, VR-4s tend to wear their somewhat expensive 17- and 18-inch tires rather quickly. The VR-4's main problem seems to stem from the Getrag transmissions, especially the later six-speed, though even the earlier five-speeds can be affected. They're often criticized for tough, chunky shifting, and they occasionally fail. Owners recommend frequent oil changes for both the transmission and differentials, with a possible switch to synthetic lubricants, as this may help. If the transmission is blown or cannot be rebuilt, figure $4,000–$5,000 plus labor. In summary, a newer, low-mileage, well-maintained example can be a great car, while an abused, high-mile fixer upper should be renamed "The Money Pit."

The 3000GT VR-4 and Dodge Stealth R/T polarize enthusiasts. Some love all the techno toys; some despise them as "mechanical Band-Aids," favoring lighter, less-complicated sports cars. Most like the styling, though many feel the earlier closed headlight cars are too busy looking with all their scoops, starches, ribs, and other details. There's no denying, however, that it's a performer in every sense of the term. A low-mileage, well-maintained example should be a very satisfying car to own if its brand of tech and performance appeals to you.

SPECIFICATIONS (1999 3000GT VR-4)

Body style. . . . . Two door, four passenger
Drivetrain layout . . . . Front engine, all-wheel-drive
Engine type. . . . . Twin-turbocharged DOHC V-6
Displacement, liter/cc 3.0/2,972
Horsepower, hp @ rpm . . . . SAE net 320 @ 6,000
Torque, ft-lb @ rpm . . . . SAE net 315 @ 2,500
Transmission . . . . 5-speed manual
Wheelbase, in.. . . . . 97.2
Length, in.. . . . . 180.7
Width, in.. . . . . 72.4
Height, in. 49.3
Base curb weight, lb 3,737
Suspension, f/r . . . . MacPherson struts, anti-roll bar/multi-link, anti-roll bar
Steering type . . . . Rack and pinion, 4-wheel steer
Brakes, f/r.. . . . . Disc/disc

PERFORMANCE

Acceleration, 0–60 mph . . . . 5.7 sec.
Standing quarter
mile, sec/mph 14.2/99.00
Source. . . . . Road & Track

TYPICAL PARTS/REPAIR PRICES

Major tune-up/service. $429
Air filter 21
Shock absorber 98
Catalytic converter(s) 169
Clutch replacement 1,300

WEBSITE

team3S.com

Chapter 18

FOR
- Sexy, Euro/Asian styling
- AWD and convertible models available
- Strong aftermarket support

AGAINST
- High care cost on AWD Turbo
- Really tight rear seat
- Chassis flex on convertible

HOT PICK
1997–1999 GS-T or GSX

REPORT CARD

Engine	B+
Transmission	B+
Power/Weight Ratio	B+
Handling	A-
Braking	B+
Ride	B+
Exterior Styling	A
Interior Styling	B+
Interior Function	B
Cargo Capacity	B
Everyday Usability	A
Reliability	A-
Fit and Finish	A-
Market Availability	A
Resale Value Potential	B
Fun Factor	B+
Bang for Buck	B+
Aftermarket Interest	A
Club Support	A

Mitsubishi Eclipse/Eagle Talon (1995–1999, 1995–1998)

Mitsubishi's racy-looking Eclipse is one of the few cars that appeals to younger, performance-savvy buyers as much the Honda Civic, Acura Integra, and Volkswagen GTI. They're fun to drive in stock form, and can be modified to crank out some serious performance by a most fervent aftermarket. Some even feel that the styling of these 1995–1999 Eclipses is even more appealing than the new-for-2000 model. While that's a personal choice, there's no denying it's a great looker against so many of the other reasonably priced offerings in the compact sport coupe class.

While some enthusiasts favor the earliest "Diamond Star" triplets (the Eclipse, Eagle Talon, and Plymouth Laser built from 1990–1994 as a joint venture between Mitsubishi and Chrysler), the last car costs so little more, it remains our pick. The Eclipse and Talon were remodeled for 1995 but the Laser was discontinued after the 1994 model year. And since the Mitsubishi Eclipse version of this platform sold in greater

Mitsubishi's second-generation Eclipse managed to employ extremely curvaceous shapes—hardly a straight line anywhere—without looking like a jellybean. This car is a top-of-the-line 1996 GSX, though it's virtually identical to what the car looked like when it came out the year before. *Mitsubishi*

It's a toss-up as to whether the Eclipse looked better or not as good after its 1997 update, but it mattered little—a great-looking car either way. A bit of the 3000GT VR-4's look crept into the front and rear fascias. Wheel treatments on this 1997 GSX were also new. *Mitsubishi*

volume and remained on the market longer, it will be the primary focus of our discussion here. Although the Mitsubishi is a Japanese nameplate, the Eclipse and Talon were both built in the Diamond Star factory in Illinois.

The second-generation Eclipse was offered in four versions: baseline GS, mid-level GS, turbocharged GS-T, and all-wheel-drive GSX. Although the RS and GS, powered by a 140-horsepower DOHC four, is a pleasant-enough piece to drive, the two turbo versions remain the enthusiast's choice. They employ a turbocharged (using Mitsubishi's own turbocharger and an intercooler to increase power and reduce engine detonation risk) DOHC 2.0-liter four that cranks out a 210-horsepower when backed by the standard five-speed manual trans, or 205-horse in four-speed automatic-equipped form. Impressive, too, is that the engine's torque peak 214–220 ft-lb of torque comes at a relatively low (for a small turbo four) 3,000 revs.

The suspension was all new for 1995 as well, employing a fully independent multilink setup front and rear; both used an upper A-arm with various horizontal and vertical links, as opposed to the more common, and cheaper, MacPherson struts. The advantage is more consistent alignment throughout the suspension's travel, resulting in a more neutral handling attitude. Front and rear anti-roll bars are part of the package. Also standard on all turbocharged versions was engine-speed-sensitive rack-and-pinion steering, four-wheel disc brakes, power windows/doors/mirrors/ locks, cruise control, air conditioning, alloy wheels, an Infinity sound system, and dual air bags.

The interior design adds to the Eclipse's racy image, and is considerably larger than that of the car it replaced. While the steeply sloped rear window somewhat minimizes rear cargo space, it's more than adequate for the class. The GSX model's full-time, all-wheel-drive system's viscous coupling manages power between the

105

One has to think Mitsu had an eye on Toyota's Supra Turbo when it developed the 1997–1999 Eclipse's rear wing; the "basket handle" look was becoming quite popular by then. Wheels are the new chrome 16-inchers, indicating this car is a 1998 model. *Mitsubishi*

Considering that a convertible model was not in mind when the second-generation Eclipse was designed, it certainly came out good. The car looks great, top up or down, and wind buffeting is commendably low. There is come cowl shake present on rough surfaces, however, and the back seat is tighter than before, but fortunately the Spyder can be had with the 210-horse turbo and is still good fun to drive. *Mitsubishi*

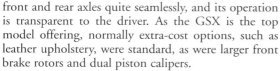

front and rear axles quite seamlessly, and its operation is transparent to the driver. As the GSX is the top model offering, normally extra-cost options, such as leather upholstery, were standard, as were larger front brake rotors and dual piston calipers.

Nineteen ninety-six saw few changes, as the car was all new just a year before. Three new colors were offered, audio systems were further upgraded as was the anti-theft system, and a leather seat option was made available that did not require the purchase of power seats on the GS-T. Since the Eclipse was (and remains) Mitsubishi's highest-volume model, little time was wasted in substantially revising it for 1997, just two years after the new platform was introduced.

Actually, 1997 began in mid-1996, as Mitsu brought out convertible versions of the GS and turbocharged GS-T, called the Eclipse Spyder. Unlike Nissan, which elected not to offer its convertible version of the 240SX with its highest horsepower engine or a manual transmission, Mitsu made the convert available in naturally aspirated and turbocharged 2wd form (however it wasn't available in awd, GSX configuration). Naturally, the hatchback bodywork gave way

to a power-folding top and a trunk, and unfortunately, rendered the back seat all but useless. The top works well, looks terrific up or down, and includes a heated glass rear window. Although Mitsubishi made the effort to stiffen the chassis to regain the structural rigidity lost by razoring away the roof, the ragtop Eclipse does suffer from a moderate amount of cowl-shake on rough surfaces. It's still an exceptionally handsome and pleasant car that performs nearly as well as the coupe, but those who value maximum handling precision will want to stick with the closed roof car.

Both front and rear fascias were revised for an even more aggressive look, the tail somewhat reminiscent of the higher performance 3000GT VR-4. The Eclipse's side cladding and rear spoiler were also redone for a crisper look. More interior and exterior colors were added, and the seat material patterns were redesigned. The GS-T got redesigned 16-inch wheels, and the top-line GSX received new 17-inch alloys. The convertibles also got the body and equipment upgrades that came along for 1997, and a standard CD player.

There must not have been too much money in the Eagle development budget, as the Talon was but a very thinly disguised Eclipse. That's nothing bad, it's just that little distinguishes the two. The Eagle will generally be cheaper to buy, but "orphan" models will also have less resale value in the future. *DaimlerChrysler*

As you'd expect, there were very few changes for 1998. The 16-inch wheels on the GS-T coupe and Spyder models were finished in chrome instead of clear-coated aluminum, and equipment levels on the GSX coupe were increased to make it a better value. That meant that a power glass moonroof, a revised leather interior with power driver seat, and a remote entry security system were all made standard. 1999 was much the same issue, with Mitsubishi again upping standard equipment levels to keep the car attractive in its fifth and final year before a remodel for 2000. The GS-T got the standard moonroof and upgraded anti-theft system this time, while the ABS and limited-slip rear differential that were options on the GSX became standard.

The Talon got a mid-life update for 1997, as did the Mitsu version, with new front fascia, new wheels, a new rear fiasco, and rear wing. However, there was no convertible version, as the Eagle Division's demise was already being planned, and there was no advantage in launching another platform variant. *DaimlerChrysler*

While the Eclipse's new wing resembled a picnic basket handle, someone once said the Talon's revised rear wing looked like an "ironing board left on the trunk." No matter, these cars are popular with the aftermarket set, and owners often do them up with body kits and the like, so Eagle and Mitsu were just getting in on the action. *DaimlerChrysler*

Debate continues to rage as to whether the front-wheel-drive GS-T or the all-wheel-drive GSX is the performance model to have. While the GSX understeers less, that is, a more predictable handler up to its limits, all-wheel-drive cars tend to break away faster once that (higher) limit is reached. In addition, the awd hardware adds weight—some 300 pounds worth, which means the GS-T is probably a tick or two faster in a straight line. The awd system also adds complexity; though the differential and associated gear have proven quite reliable, they represent a cost and maintenance issue that will have to be dealt with as the car ages. Best bet: drive both, and see which suits your driving style the best, and if you do elect to pursue a GSX, look for, and pay extra for, a very low-mileage example.

The Eclipse is a well-built, nicely finished, and generally reliable car, but not without its foibles. A rough idle, when cold, very hot, or after hard acceleration or deceleration, is not uncommon, and can be attributed to one of several engine management system problems—all diagnosable, and all relatively easy to fix, but again, perhaps more common than with other cars. Transmissions will wear given constant hard use, starting with the second-gear synchro (worn by aggressive 1-2 shifts), and problems with the wastegate, or blow-off valve, in the turbo systems are also not uncommon.

The transfer/diff case on GSX's can leak fluid, and ultimately overheat and fail; this was a recall item, and can be addressed by a dealer if it hasn't been already. A review of owner group websites also evidences a propensity for problems with the power window mechanisms. Also important is the condition of the turbo; if the car you're looking at has 75,000 or more miles, a new or rebuilt turbo is in its near future, unless it's been given religious oil changes and exceptional care. Figure $1,000 for a rebuilt unit, plus labor.

As mentioned, Chrysler's short-lived Eagle division also sold a version of the Eclipse called the Talon. The 2wd Turbo version is called the TSi, and the awd is called (logically enough) the TSi AWD. Although hardcore Eagleites will swear that they are really very different cars, they're not. Equipment and option packaging differed slightly, as of course did color offerings and the like. The Talon got its own rear window treatment, and front/rear fascia designs. By the time the convertible body style showed up, the Eagle nameplate's days were numbered, so the Talon was never offered as a Spyder, though it also received the freshening that the Eclipse got for 1997. 1998 was the last year for the Talon, and for Eagle. There's no mechanical reason not to consider one, and some may even prefer it for style or rarity's sake. It may also be cheaper than a similar Eclipse. But the fact that it's a now-defunct model from a now-defunct nameplate makes it less desirable than the Mitsubishi version of the same car, unless the deal is way, way too good to pass up.

Great styling, worthy handling, high equipment levels, 200+ horsepower, and the availability of all-wheel-drive or a convertible have to make the 1995–1999 turbocharged Eclipse one of the strongest, if not always the cheapest, buys in this book.

SPECIFICATIONS (1999 GS-T)

Body style. . . . . Two door, four passenger
Drivetrain layout. . . . . Front engine, front drive
Engine type . . . . DOHC Turbocharged inline four, cast-iron block, aluminum head
Displacement, liter/cc 2.0/1,996
Horsepower, hp @ rpm . . . . SAE net 210 @ 6,000
Torque, ft-lb @ rpm . . . . SAE net 214 @ 3,000
Transmission . . . . 5-speed manual
Wheelbase, in.. . . . . 98.8
Length, in. 172.4
Width, in.. . . . . 68.3
Height, in. 49.8
Base curb weight, lb 2,970
Suspension, f/r . . . . Upper A-arm, links, anti-roll bar/upper A-arm, links, anti-roll bar
Steering type. . . . . Rack and pinion
Brakes, f/r . . . . Disc/disc

PERFORMANCE (1996 GSX)

Acceleration, 0–60 mph . . . . 7.0 sec.
Standing quarter
mile, sec/mph 15.4/89.0
Source. . . . . Road & Track

TYPICAL PARTS/REPAIR PRICES

Major tune-up/service. $390
Air filter 17
Shock absorber 101
Catalytic converter(s) 129
Clutch replacement 675

WEBSITES

eclipse.com
dsm.org

Chapter 19

FOR
- Early and later version is a good looker
- Rear-drive platform, rear-drive handling
- Reasonably priced

AGAINST
- No top-line V-6 or turbo version
- 2.4-liter four a bit boomy
- 1997 restyle a bit overdone

HOT PICK
1991–1994 SE Fastback (w/five-speed and handling package)

REPORT CARD

Engine . . . . .B
Transmission . . . . .B-
Power/Weight Ratio . . . . .B
Handling . . . . .A-
Braking . . . . .B
Ride . . . . .B+
Exterior Styling . . . . . . .B
Interior Styling . . . . .B
Interior Function . . . . . .B+
Cargo Capacity . . . . . . .B+
Everyday Usability . . . . .A-
Reliability . . . . .A-
Fit and Finsh . . . . .A-
Market Availability . . . . .B
Resale Value Potential . . .B+
Fun Factor . . . . .B
Bang for Buck . . . . .B
Aftermarket Interest . . . .B+
Club Support . . . . .B+

Nissan 240SX
(1990–1998)

Nissan brought out the 240SX in 1989 in an attempt to recapture some of the simple sports car values that made the original 240Z so popular. By the late 1980s, what was by then the 300ZX had gone way upmarket, in terms of specifications and price, and was about to go up a step further for 1990. So Nissan created another 240. Some of the supposed connection to the original was a bit of marketing spin—a six-cylinder, two-seater sports car as opposed to the 240SX being a four-cylinder 2+2 hatchback or notchback—but none of that took away from the new 240's rear-wheel-drive appeal and excellent handling. This platform, internally dubbed S13, was originally launched with a 2.4-liter SOHC four good for 140 horsepower; the 1990 car was virtually unchanged.

Nissan's straightforward, bullet-nose-shaped 240SX was a proverbial breath of fresh air after some of the gimmicky-styled Japanese cars of the 1980s. Best one to get is the SE version with the optional handling package, though even the base car can be made to handle well with a little help from the aftermarket. *Nissan*

The notchback or two-door sedan versions of most models are often less attractive than the racier fastbacks. But that doesn't necessarily apply to the 240SX. Some people prefer a conventional trunk, and these cars are a bargain in the marketplace today. *Nissan*

As noted, the 240SX is a rear-drive car in what was already becoming a front-drive world, so that alone gives it value to those who prefer the torque steer-free handling characteristics of a rear driver. It was initially offered in two body styles, a notchback coupe with a conventional trunk, and a racier hatchback version. Both cars were offered in base and SE versions, plus the fastback could be had in high-line LE trim.

The 240SX cost a bit more than some of the other sporty coupes of the early 1990s, but packed in a lot of value. The suspension was fully independent, using a modified strut/lower control arm system up front, and Nissan's own multilink, independent setup out back. Standard fare included power rack-and-pinion steering, four-wheel disc brakes, full instrumentation, AM/FM/cassette, dual power mirrors, and a host of other goodies that were often optional on other machines. A five-speed manual transmission was standard, with a four-speed automatic being optional; other extras included air conditioning, leather interior

trim, power windows, ABS, and the like. The interior design is clean and straightforward, except for the gimmicky heads-up/digital instrument display that later showed up on the coupe version, with at least reasonable rear-seat room, and the fastback has more cargo capacity than a 300ZX.

Although 240SX boffins like these original 1989–1990 cars, Nissan stepped up the performance pace for 1991. The single-cam, 12-valve engine cylinder head went away in favor of a new, double-overhead cam, four-valves-per-cylinder unit (the rest of the engine's basic architecture was essentially unchanged). The result was an increase of 15 horsepower (to 155), and torque increased from 152 ft-lb to an even 160. Although these don't seem like big numbers, they translated to considerably improved acceleration: *Motor Trend* tested a 1991 to a 0–60 time of 8.0 seconds, as opposed to 9.5 for an also-five-speed-equipped 1989. Also of interest to the enthusiast driver was the addition of an optional handling package, available only on SE

The 1994 240SX Convertible is certainly handsome enough, but was only offered with an automatic transmission, and without the availability of the handling package option. Unless you just want a convertible, enthusiast drivers will avoid this model—you'd spend a lot of money trying to make it really perform. *Nissan*

Fastbacks, which included a version of the Super HICAS four-wheel steering system found on the 300ZX Turbo. The package also included larger wheels and tires, sport-tuned shocks and springs, and a viscous limited-slip differential. If you are interested in a 1991–1994 240, it's worth seeking one out that has this package. Other changes for 1991 included a revised front fascia, and the 240SX went into 1992 unchanged with exception of a new color.

Nineteen ninety-three seemed to be the year for convertibles at Nissan, as the 300ZX and 240SX showed up that year with newly available open-air body styles. The 240's power-operated (the 300's is manual!) top stowed beneath a plastic tonneau cover. Nice cruiser though it is, the 240SX convertible was not aimed at the sports car types: it was only offered with an automatic transmission and was not offered with the handling package. The rest of the 240 lineup remained unchanged, save for the phase-in of 134a refrigerant AC systems during the model year and the offering of new exterior colors.

Nineteen ninety-four was the swan song for the first-generation 240SX, and it continued with only minor equipment reshuffling to make it a slightly better value in its last year on the market. But big changes

were on the way for 1995 in the form of a complete redo (carrying the internal designation S14) and a change in focus at the same time. Nissan's own press release for the newly designed 1995 240SX commented that "the age of buyers of these vehicles is shifting upward on average, and that they have greater expectations for comfort, convenience, and safety, and less desire for flashy 'boy racer' styling." This was an unusual statement, as the previous 240 was often praised for its clean, relatively unadorned look particularly in fastback form. Nonetheless, Nissan re-dealt the 240's deck in the form of an elegant-looking coupe, while the fastback version bit the dust.

Given the upscale target nature of the 1995 240, a considerable amount of effort was made to reduce noise, vibration, and harshness: new intake system baffles, engine mounts, more sound insulation, and other measures did result in a quieter, suppler Z. Unfortunately, the demise of the fastback body style took the handling package and four-wheel steering system with it, though the SE still represented a sportier suspension setup than the base version and included 16-inch wheels. The new chassis benefited from improved structural integrity, with a 50 percent increase in torsional rigidity and a 100 percent increase in bending

The hatchback and convert went away as part of the 1995 240SX's redesign, though one can hardly complain about the appearance of the coupe, especially in SE form. A good number of hardware pieces got left off, such as the more sophisticated multilink rear axle, and the new car gained a few pounds, but the structure is stiffer, so it still makes a reasonable basis for a performance machine. *Nissan*

rigidity. The wheelbase increased by 50 millimeters over the previous version, and the new car was a bit wider, though overall length remained about the same.

To most eyes, the new interior represented an improvement; an even more businesslike dash design, higher quality materials, and even better fit and finish than the previous car, and the slightly longer wheelbase yielded a minor improvement in terms of rear-seat legroom. The SE version also got white-faced gauges, and dual air bags were now standard on all 240SXs.

For some reason, Nissan only waited a year to fiddle with the front grille design, as it was changed slightly for 1996. Other changes for that year were new seat cloth and a juggling of options and option package availability. Apparently, buyers began to miss some of that recently dumped "boy racer" image, so the 240 received a mid-life facelift for 1997 in the form of a more aggressive front fascia, "ground effects" style rocker panel extension, and minor changes to the rear-end styling to make it look sportier.

Did it work? To most eyes, no—as the pieces just looked too added-on, cluttering up the previous car's nice shape and clean detailing. But that, of course, is a matter of personal choice. The 240SX's last year, 1998, brought no substantive changes.

We've driven both early and late 240s, and prefer the 1991–1994 SE version with or without the handling suspension option. The engine is not particularly smooth or quiet, and doesn't rev as happily as do most of the Honda and Toyota fours, but it does put out admirable power, and the chassis is more than up to the job. Its handling attitude is very neutral, progressing toward understeer only as the limit is neared, and only then when pushed. The steering offers good road feel, the brakes stop surely and with a firm pedal, and body roll is reasonably well checked. Although the leather interior is certainly attractive, some actually prefer the standard cloth, as it grips better during hard cornering. These cars came with what would now be viewed as pretty modest rolling stock, and they really

Was the 240SX's mid-life, "boy racer" facelift a success? That's a matter of personal taste, but apparently it failed to catch enough buyers to survive past the 1998 model year. The late 1990s were tough times for Nissan, as within a four-model-year time period, the 300ZX, Sentra SE-R, 240SX SE, and 200SX SE-R all bit the dust. Fortunately, there are a ton of them out there in the used car marketplace. *Nissan*

respond to more aggressive 16- or even 17-inch wheels and modern performance rubber (though don't overdo it). And even though we said that an SE with the handling package is worth looking for, its abilities (with the exception of the four-wheel steering system) can be easily and inexpensively duplicated—or bettered—in the aftermarket.

The 1995–1998 is a pleasant and still sporty car, though it's not nearly as edgy feeling as the earlier one. It is quieter, both from an engine and a road noise standpoint, and the later interior is certainly a comfy place to be. But the newer car doesn't feel as reactive or athletic—a shame, as the structurally stiffer structure should have been an even better foundation for a serious performance machine. Whether you choose an early or late version 240, we strongly suggest you stick with the SE model equipped with the five-speed. You'll spend more bringing a base version up to its equipment and suspension levels, and the automatic turns the car into more of a commuter than a canyon carver.

Both generations of 240SX have proven extremely reliable cars. The earliest (1989–1990) suffered some engine maladies that were well corrected by the time the DOHC version of the 2.4 engine came along, so

for that reason alone, we'd recommend a 1991 or later car. Rough idle problems occasionally plague the 1989–1994 cars, though this is usually the adjustment or simple replacement of the idle control unit. Other elements and sensors belonging to the electronic engine system are prone to failure, though some cars will go forever without a single one going south. The first-gen cars had pop-up headlights, and those units are prone to sticking once in a while; a clean/oil/adjust of the mechanism usually solves it.

AC units on the 1989–1994 cars are sometimes problematic, as are the seals around the sunroofs, which when damaged or dried out can cause leakage. The rear suspension bushings on any 240SX can wear with age, causing improper alignment and sagging; plan on spending some money in this area on any car with 100,000 or more on it. The basic engine/clutch/transmission/rear end is very tough, and a review of club websites evidence many members' cars with 150,000–200,000 miles on them still going strong.

If you're looking for a fine-handling, rear-wheel-drive alternative to all the small fwd coupes out there, the 240SX—particularly those 1991–1994 models—offer a reliable, attractively priced option.

SPECIFICATIONS (1991 SE SPORT PACKAGE)

Body style. . . . . Two door, four passenger
Drivetrain layout. . . . . Front engine, front drive
Engine type. DOHC inline four, aluminum block and head
Displacement, liter/cc 2.4/2,389
Horsepower, hp @ rpm . . . . SAE net 155 @ 5,600
Torque, ft-lb @ rpm . . . . SAE net 160 @ 4,400
Transmission . . . . 5-speed manual
Wheelbase, in. 97.4
Length, in. 178.0
Width, in. 66.5
Height, in. 50.8
Base curb weight, lb 2,747
Suspension, f/r . . . . MacPherson strut/multilink
Steering type. . . . . Rack and pinion
Brakes, f/r . . . . Disc/disc

PERFORMANCE

Acceleration, 0–60 mph . . . . 8.0 sec.
Standing quarter
mile, sec/mph 16.1/86.7
Source . . . . Motor Trend

TYPICAL PARTS/REPAIR PRICES

Major tune-up/service. $250
Air filter 7
Shock absorber 104
Catalytic converter(s) 107
Clutch replacement 750

WEBSITES

240sx.org
nav.webring.yahoo.com/hub?ring=nissan&list

Nissan 300ZX
(1990–1996)

REPORT CARD

Engine	A
Transmission	A
Power/Weight Ratio	A-
Handling	A
Braking	B+
Ride	B+
Exterior Styling	B-
Interior Styling	B-
Interior Function	B
Cargo Capacity	B
Everyday Usability	B+
Reliability	B+
Fit and Finish	A-
Market Availability	B-
Resale Value Potential	A-
Fun Factor	A-
Bang for Buck	A
Aftermarket Interest	B
Club Support	A-

The Nissan 300ZX is arguably one of the best sports and GT cars of the 1990s. Both sports and GT? Yes: in short, two-seat, manual transmission, and especially twin-turbo form, it's a sports car (a large one, but a sports car for sure). In 2+2, automatic guise, it's a Grand Tourer. It's got style, it's well built, was produced in adequate numbers to ensure a reasonable supply, and works as an everyday ride. Typical competitors include the rest of the "300 Horsepower Club" of the day: Chevrolet Corvette, Toyota Supra, and the Mitsubishi 3000GT VR-4/Dodge Stealth.

Save the V-6 engine block, the fourth-generation "big Z" was an all-new car when it was launched in 1990, and as such garnered *Motor Trend's* Import Car of the Year award. It was also an amazingly complete line of sports cars: there were two different wheelbases (two-seater and 2+2), both with a naturally aspirated V-6 3.0-liter DOHC engine, and either of which could be had with a five-speed manual or four-speed

Not everyone was a fan of the Z's all-new look for 1990, though it's certainly aggressive and wore the test of time fairly well. Nobody, however, complained about its chassis dynamics or V-6 powertrains. This is a 1990 two-seater. *Nissan*

1991 brought very few visible changes, though one minor one was to remove the Nissan script from the bumper, in favor of the chrome-ringed badge still in use today. Coupe and 2+2 models look much the same, although the 2+2 is visibly longer between the wheels, due to its 6-inch-wheelbase increase. *Nissan*

automatic. The two-seater was additionally available as the 300ZX Turbo, packing a twin-turbocharged, 300-horsepower version of the V-6. Both body styles came with standard, removable glass "T-tops."

Japanese cars were all about high technology in the late 1980s and early 1990s, and the 300ZX was no exception, with the real techno tour de force being the turbo model: Besides cranking 300 horsepower (280 when mated with the automatic) out of 3.0 liters through the use of twin turbos and dual intercoolers, dual overhead cams, and four-valve-per-cylinder heads with variable valve timing, the Z packed a fully independent suspension, ABS brakes (not yet so common in 1990), a limited-slip differential, and a full complement of power assists. Its main "gee whiz" calling card was called Super HICAS, which was in effect an electronically controlled four-wheel steer system. Its acceleration, handling, braking, and other performance numbers were as good as any of the cars in its competitive set and are still impressive today.

This is not to sell short the naturally aspirated version either, which employs a non-turbo version of the same 3.0-liter, DOHC V-6. It's good for a worthy 222 horsepower—about as much as the 5.0-liter Mustang of the day, though it's nearly 100 ft-lb short in the torque department—and should not be ruled out as a worthy performance alternative. A few Z experts actually rate a short-wheelbase, two-seat, fixed roof, naturally aspirated five-speed 300ZX as the sportiest of the bunch, though it doesn't quite pack the punch of the turbo version. Bolt on aftermarket intake and exhaust systems, plus perhaps a high-performance engine control module, and it's an honest 250 horsepower sports car, without the hassle and expense of turbos.

The 300ZX cabin is a hospitable place, if not quite as businesslike as that of, say, the Mazda RX-7. Nissan has always gone for lots of lights and unusual control styles: the 300ZX placed several of the ancillary controls on stalks placed either side of the main instrument binnacle. Easy to reach, but not necessarily intuitive to use. For example, the fan switch for the standard automatic AC/climate control system is sequential, meaning if it's set on "2" and you want "1," you have to cycle through "3" and "4" to get there. But the main gauges are easy to see, the seats comfortable and supportive, and the rear cargo area will swallow a reasonable, if not considerable, amount of cargo. Cloth and vinyl seat trim were standard, and leather was optional. The 2+2 model had even more room inside for the tallest of drivers, though the rear seats should be considered vestigial at best. Cruise control, plus power windows, locks, and mirrors, was also standard.

The three gills on the lower front fascia give away this 1992 as a 300ZX Turbo. Another visual clue is the rear deck-mounted spoiler. *Nissan*

117

Nissan got the ZX right just about from the beginning, and it saw amazingly few updates throughout its seven-model-year lifespan. A non-T-top two-seater version showed up for 1991, as did a standard Bose audio system (with optional CD) on Turbo and 2+2 models; the driver-side air bag that was optional for 1991 became standard in 1992. 1992 also brought upgraded standard cloth upholstery, a standard power driver seat (on all but the nat-asp two-seater), and leather trim on the automatic trans shifter.

Big news came in 1993, in the form of yet another body style in addition to the two-seat and 2+2 coupe versions: a two-seat convertible, built on the short wheelbase platform. The top system was unusual in that it employed a chassis-stiffening bar that looks for all the world like a roll bar, though Nissan materials never called it that. The canvas top was a manual unit, and fit neatly beneath a hard plastic tonneau cover. What was a hatch out back became a more conventional trunk. As the convert still doesn't possess quite the structural integrity of a coupe, and therefore not quite as precise a platform for high-speed handling, the 300ZX Convertible was only offered in naturally aspirated form, with either the five-speed stick or automatic transmission. It isn't as stylish as the swoopy coupe, but the appeal of driving al fresco is attractive.

Nineteen ninety-four was another year of few changes, with a standard passenger-side air bag being the only notable revision. As the Z was offered in so many variations, there was little left to do short of a

This 1994 shows the rear deck spoiler. The original five "twisted spoke" wheel design still looked good, and amazingly stayed with the car its entire production life. *David Newhardt*

full redesign, and as prices had climbed and sales had begun to taper off, 1995 and 1996 were essentially carryover years, save for a little color combo shuffling.

The big thing to watch out for when considering a 300ZX turbo is, of course, that wonderful 100-horsepower-per-liter twin-turbo V-6. By now, you're probably tired of hearing that oil changes are critical in any engine, but they're more important in the case of a turbocharged one, and doubly important when two turbos are involved. Blow up this engine, and you're looking at around $7,500 for a complete rebuild, assuming you redo both turbos at the same time. Turbo replacements by themselves run $1,500 each, perhaps less if you can get the unit rebuilt. A major tune-up and timing belt replacement are required every 60,000 miles; experts recommend replacing the water pump at the same time—the total for these three items shouldn't run over $1,000. Otherwise, the engines are tough, and should prove trouble free: 150,000 of service out of a well-maintained turbo V-6 is possible, and the naturally aspirated version can go 200K+ before it needs to be opened up for major work.

Both transmissions are more than tough enough to handle the non-turbo V-6, though the Turbo version is a lot stronger and will wear them out if the car's been driven hard. Neither will last much beyond 100,000 miles on Turbos, and don't expect more than 75,000–80,000 miles out of a Turbo clutch either. The driveshaft is a two-piece unit with a U-joint in the middle; a rumbling and grumbling sound while under way could indicate this unit has packed up, a worn transmission mount, or both. Fortunately, neither is difficult nor expensive to replace.

The convertible version of the 300ZX is a bit of a paradox. The notion of the Z's driving experience enhanced by letting the sun shine in is appealing. The somewhat ungainly chassis-stiffening brace that arcs its way across the passenger compartment is less so. Some also resented a fully manual top in a car this expensive. *Nissan*

Nissan did its best to bank the current Z off the heritage established by the original, but all that did was to underscore the questionable move of killing the car off after the 1996 model year. Here, a final-year 1996 poses with an original 240Z of 1991. *Nissan*

Note that the factory wheels, which are sort of a five-spoke, fan-shaped affair, are designed to cool the brakes and only work in one direction. In other words, there are right-side and left-side wheels, and they should not be swapped side for side. The rear suspension is mounted in a subframe that involves four sophisticated silicone-filled mounts; as these wear, or break and leak, they'll cause the rear suspension to get sloppy and possibly sag. Replacing the whole system runs about $1,000.

T-tops and side windows may leak or allow excessive wind noise, but it's probably not from bad rubber

From the rear, the Z looks husky and purposeful, though the rear cargo area doesn't hold as much as you might think from the look of it. This is a 1996 model Z Turbo. *Nissan*

This shot offers a good look at the Z's glass T-roofs, in this case on a 1994 turbo. They did cost the Z a minimum amount of structural rigidity, but not much, and are a worthy compromise if you want a semi-convertible experience. *David Newhardt*

The Z cabin changed little over the years. Not everyone liked the controls that flanked the main instrument binnacle, and some of the displays look a bit overdone these days. Still, a comfortable place in which to drive. *David Newhardt*

seals. There are adjustments for both, and this should take care of the problem unless the seals are obviously worn or torn. Brake rotors tend to warp and/or wear out quickly, so count on every other brake job including replacement rotors.

The 300ZX left the marketplace after the 1996 model year for several reasons, though virtually none of them had anything to do with relative goodness of the car itself: the rising yen had made it awfully pricey for a then-seven-year-old design, and the market was being pummeled with new offerings: Porsche Boxster, Mercedes SLK, the C5 Corvette, and the BMW Z3, to name a few. Nissan didn't have the money for the complete redesign the Z would have needed to stay competitive, so unfortunately, it followed its Japanese cousins, Mazda's RX-7 and Toyota's MR2 and Supra, into the abyss. But none of that keeps the Z from being a great used sports car choice.

SPECIFICATIONS (1995 TURBO)

Body style. . . . . Two door, two passenger
Drivetrain layout . . . . Front engine, rear drive
Engine type . . . . Twin-turbo DOHC V-6
Displacement, liter/cc 3.0/2,996
Horsepower, hp @ rpm SAE net 300 @ 6,400
Torque, ft-lb @ rpm . . . . SAE net 283 @ 3,600
Transmission . . . . 5-speed manual
Wheelbase, in.. . . . . 96.5
Length, in.. . . . . 169.5
Width, in.. . . . . 70.5
Height, in. 49.2
Base curb weight, lb 3,480
Suspension, f/r . . . . Upper and lower control arms/multilink
Steering type. . . . . Rack and pinion
Brakes, f/r . . . . disc/disc

PERFORMANCE

Acceleration, 0–60 mph . . . . 5.5 sec.
Standing quarter
mile, sec/mph 14.4/99.7
Source . . . . Motor Trend

TYPICAL PARTS/REPAIR PRICES

Major tune-up/service. $290
Air filter 13
Shock absorber 76
Catalytic converter(s) 148
Clutch replacement 1,040

WEBSITES

twinturbo.com
zcar.com
autoforums.com/twinturbo

Chapter 21

Nissan Sentra SE-R/200SX SE-R (1991–1994, 1995–1998)

FOR
- Good performance/ dollar ratio
- Sleeper looks
- Adequate supply

AGAINST
- Engine not particularly smooth
- Low-mile Sentra SE-R's becoming tough to find
- Sleeper looks not to everyone's taste

HOT PICK
1993 Sentra SE-R

REPORT CARD

Engine	B+
Transmission	B+
Power/Weight Ratio	B+
Handling	B+
Braking	B+
Ride	B
Exterior Styling	B
Interior Styling	B
Interior Function	B+
Cargo Capacity	B+
Everyday Usability	A-
Reliability	A-
Fit and Finish	A-
Market Availability	A-
Resale Value Potential	A
Fun Factor	A-
Bang for Buck	A
Aftermarket Interest	B+
Club Support	B+

Nissan certainly knew how to deliver a high-performance, low-cost, compact two-door during the 1990s: it marketed three Sentra-based models alone from 1990 to 1999. Although the beady-eyed NX2000 that was a product of the late 1980s (lasting through 1993) was a quirky-fun, 140-horsepower hatchback, the notion of low-buck Nissan performance really caught stride with the launch of the Sentra SE-R in 1991. The Sentra was all new that year, and the SE-R is the performance version; the plebeian E, XE, and SE need not be considered in your hunt for a low-buck pocket rocket. The SE-R recaptured much of the boxy, compact performance sedan magic that had been missing since the original—and oft-race winning—Datsun 510 of the late 1960s/early 1970s.

Although the basic platform was very much standard Sentra, Nissan packed in the best goodies it could find in the parts bin: a high-revving, all-alloy, 140-horsepower 2.0-liter DOHC four; a close ratio five-speed manual transmission; a well-calibrated fully independent sport suspension;

Squint at the Sentra SE-R, and you can see more than a bit of Nissan's original shoebox mini-rocket, the Datsun 510 of the late 1960s-early 1970s. And it wasn't just looks, as the SE-R included the 140-horsepower 2.0-liter that wasn't offered in other Sentra models. *Nissan*

Another formula for performance that the SE-R brings to mind is that of the original Pontiac GTO. Take one relatively lightweight, midsize body shell, stuff in a larger engine, give it some suspension tweaks to upgrade the handling, and boom: instant musclecar, or in this case, econo musclecar. *Nissan*

alloy wheels, limited-slip differential; sports seats; full instrumentation; monochromatic paint scheme; AM/FM/cassette; tilt wheel; power rack-and-pinion steering; and a rear deck lid–mounted wing. In order to keep the price low, there were few high-buck, weight-adding options: upgraded sound systems, AC, ABS, a moonroof, and some leather trim for the shifter and steering wheel knob—that's about it. It is hard to imagine a more no-nonsense package than this.

And it worked. During the early 1970s, the Datsun 510 was referred to as "a poor man's BMW 2002." Two decades later, the tables had turned, as an SE-R would handily outrun the much costlier BMW 318is, prompting one journalist of the day to opine that "the BMW 318 has become the rich man's Sentra SE-R." Various car magazines got 0–60 times ranging from the low 7-second range to about 8.1—pretty impressive for a car that cost around $12,000. The engine redlines at a lofty 7,500 rpm, though isn't as smooth as competitive Honda and Acura fours.

The SE-R handles, too: we've tested them, and enjoy the light steering that retains acceptable road feel and the relative tautness of the suspension. The standard 14-inch rolling stock is a bit puny by today's standards, but that's easily addressed in the aftermarket. The SE-R is also a practical beast too: after all, it is still just a Sentra, so it's easy to drive, will carry back-seat passengers in more comfort than many smaller hatchbacks, has an adequate trunk, and earns a non-sports car insurance rating. Braking is adequate, though we recommend an ABS-equipped car if you can find one.

Relatively few changes were made throughout the SE-R's all-too-short life. 1992 SE-Rs are virtually identical to 1991, with the exception of cruise control being offered as an option. The SE-R did receive the expected mid-life update for 1993, in the form of a

more aggressive front fascia with integrated driving lights and a slightly revised grille; much of the lower body trim that was previously black was now finished in body color. The speedo and tach swapped spots, and the temp and fuel gauge orientation was also changed. The rear finisher panel, between the taillights, was made wider. There were new seat fabrics, the previously optional leather steering wheel was made standard, and a driver's-side airbag showed up on the option list. It was a subtle, yet effective round of changes, and even in its third year, enthusiast magazines were still giddy about the SE-R price/value/performance equation. 1994, the Sentra SE-R's last, was virtually a carryover year, save for revised exhaust cam timing that resulted in a slight loss of power (according to www.SE-R.net) though we've not been able to verify this through Nissan's own materials.

1993 brought subtle changes inside and out, the most easily spotted from outside being that much of what was black trim before was now finished in body color. Still, the SE-R's appearance was so innocuous, few ticket writers paid attention. *Nissan*

Enthusiasts were concerned that the demise of the Sentra SE-R would bring an end to low-buck performance cars from Nissan, but not so; the spirit, if not the exact execution, of the hottest Sentra lived on in the 200SX SE-R. The SE-R treatment was much the same for the 200SX as it was for the Sentra, including upgraded suspension, alloy wheels, fog lights, a rear wing, and most importantly, the 140-horse 2.0-liter engine. In spite of the fact that it might have looked a bit racier than the Sentra, the 200SX didn't catch the imagination of enthusiasts to the extent that the earlier "shoebox" did, though it's just as fun to drive. *Nissan*

The Sentra was remodeled for 1995, and the coupe versions were renamed 200SX in an attempt to relate it to the higher performance, higher cost 240SX and 300ZX models. Thankfully, an SE-R version remained in the lineup. Even though the new car had a demi-fastback look, it still employed a conventional trunk as opposed to a hatchback body style. Although the 200SX SE-R retained the same 2.0-liter DOHC four—even the power ratings remained unchanged—it was a bit of a mixed blessing. Good in the sense that certain feature levels went up: a bit more room in back, a bit more cargo space, larger 15-inch alloy wheels, and dual front air bags standard as standard equipment. But enthusiasts were less than impressed with the addition of a less costly, and somewhat less sophisticated beam rear axle arrangement instead of the previous multilink setup. While this simpler system supposedly made for a quieter ride and will probably require less maintenance in the long run, it just isn't quite as sharp from a handling standpoint. Fortunately, front and rear anti-roll bars, four-wheel disc brakes with optional ABS, and the viscous limited-slip diff remained.

Like the Sentra SE-R, the 200SX SE-R lived a four-year production life. 1994 brought only a bit of color shuffling, and 1997 yet some more. Furthermore, the 200SX SE-R was not offered in California due to it not meeting emissions requirements. Curiously, the entire 200SX lineup was given a fairly substantial round of updates for 1998—its last year on the market—which leads us to believe that perhaps Nissan had plans to keep this sporty coupe around another year, then killed it off at the last minute. In any case, there were new front and rear fascias, new headlights, grille, and taillights, plus new standard cloth upholstery. Some of the exterior elements that were previously chrome were now finished in body color or black, and the engine was re-certified for sale in all 50 states. The dash got white-face gauges, the sunroof became standard, and the limited-slip differential was dropped.

Both the Sentra SE-R and 200SX SE-R are straightforward and reliable cars, but as always, there are things to watch out for. The earliest 1991 was known for difficult shift effort, but that certainly wasn't the only transmission issue: the five-speed trannies in all 1991–1994 SE-Rs have a reputation for popping out of fifth gear (this was apparently fixed on the 200SX SE-R). The SE-R clubs have the fix well documented, and it doesn't affect every car but is a well-known problem. The starter also seems to be a weak link; it squeals when worn but is easily and inexpensively replaced, and again the Nissan specialists have heavy-duty starters that cure the problem for good.

Early Sentra SE-R's occasionally suffer fuel pump failure, and the HVAC switch and/or relay occasionally fails to where it will only work on the highest setting. As noted, the rear multilink suspension on the Sentra SE-R has many bushings, and as they age (nearing 100,000 miles), rear-end alignment gets sloppy, handling deteriorates, and tire wear increases. Replacing all these eight bushings, plus the anti-roll bar bushings, makes it good as new. The engine is as tough as nails, basic build and finish quality on all models is reasonable, there's an enthusiastic owners' club and aftermarket base—and the price is right.

SPECIFICATIONS (1991 SENTRA SE-R)

Body style	Two door, four passenger
Drivetrain layout	Front engine, front drive
Engine type	DOHC I-4
Displacement, liter/cc	2.0-liter/1,998 cc
Horsepower, hp @ rpm	SAE net 140 @ 6,400
Torque, ft-lb @ rpm	SAE net 132 @ 4,800
Transmission	5-speed manual
Wheelbase, in.	95.7
Length, in.	170.3
Width, in.	65.6
Height, in.	53.9
Base curb weight, lb	2,594
Suspension, f/r	MacPherson strut, anti-roll bar/multilink, anti-roll bar
Steering type	Rack and pinion
Brakes, f/r	Disc/disc

PERFORMANCE

Acceleration, 0–60 mph	8.1 sec.
Standing quarter mile, sec/mph	16.2/87.0
Source	Road & Track

TYPICAL PARTS/REPAIR PRICES

Major tune-up/service	$469
Air filter	7
Shock absorber	130
Catalytic converter(s)	107
Clutch replacement	475

WEBSITE

se-r.net

Chapter 22

FOR
- Big, American-style V-8 power
- Swoopy styling
- Performance/value ratio

AGAINST
- Fit and finish not up to Euro/Asian standards
- Back seat really cramped
- Loves gas

HOT PICK
1998 Trans Am WS-6

REPORT CARD

Engine	A
Transmission	A
Power/Weight Ratio	A
Handling	B-
Braking	B-
Ride	B-
Exterior Styling	A
Interior Styling	C+
Interior Function	C-
Cargo Capacity	C-
Everyday Usability	B
Reliability	B
Fit and Finsh	C
Market Availability	A-
Resale Value Potential	B-
Fun Factor	A-
Bang for Buck	A-
Aftermarket Interest	A-
Club Support	B

Pontiac Firebird Trans Am/Formula (1993–1999)

In the beginning (circa 1967), Pontiac's Firebird and Chevrolet's Camaro were very different cars. Not so much in terms of body and chassis, as the Camaro and Firebird have been platform mates since the early days. But Firebirds had Pontiac engines, and Camaros were powered by Chevrolet powerplants. In the 1970s, division-specific engines began going the way of the Dodo bird. From a production and cost standpoint, it sort of makes sense: why did Chevrolet, Pontiac, Buick, and Oldsmobile all need to tool and produce different 350-ci V-8 engines?

What we're getting at here is that other than the look of their nose, tail, and trim, the Pontiac Firebird and Chevrolet Camaro are *essentially* the same car. There are certain differences in options or option packages and perhaps in the way some of the suspension tuning is done; but otherwise, what goes for one, goes for the other—especially with reference

By the time the Firebird's 1993 redesign came along, the famous "bird beak" look that had been with the car for more than 25 years was gone, replaced with this somewhat featureless prow dominated by large driving lights. This is a 1996 Trans Am, with the WS-6 Ram Air package. This SLP-developed option was certainly not just for looks, and represented a genuine horsepower increase. *Pontiac*

The use of a "Honeycomb" theme one place or another has been a Pontiac styling cue for decades, and shows up here in the rear lighting fascia. This is a 1998 Trans Am, the first to carry the new-generation, all-aluminum LS1 engines. They may or may not have yet slipped in under our $20,000 price ceiling, but they will soon, and represent genuine performance for money.

to the current, post-1993 genre. The last Firebird to carry a powertrain different from that of a Camaro was the 20th Anniversary Edition of 1989. And even that engine—all 250 (conservatively rated) horsepower of it—was borrowed from Buick!

Performance enthusiasts will want to concentrate on the V-8-powered 'Bird, and that means either the Formula model or the Trans Am. Again, both are essentially the same, though the Trans Am carries more aggressively straked, winged, and cladded bodywork. Some actually like the look of the simpler Formula better, though the TA certainly carries the musclecar nameplate, which itself came from the SCCA racing series called the Trans-Am.

From their introduction in 1993 through the 1997 model year, both the Trans Am and Formula could be had with Chevy's LT1 V-8, initially rated at 275 horsepower; output was upped to 285 for 1996. Take your choice between GM's excellent four-speed overdrive automatic or a Borg-Warner T-56 six-speed manual, the latter of which was somewhat rare for the first year or so due to limited supply.

The Firebird benefited from the same chassis and powertrain upgrades that the Camaro got for 1998. Most notable was the new 305-horse, all-aluminum LS1 V-8 engines, improved brakes, and a myriad of minor quality improvements. These changes would carry the car through the balance of the decade. Not to

Many prefer the Firebird Formula model's cleaner look to that of the Trans Am. It's true there's less side cladding and less aggressive nose treatments but no less horsepower, and the suspension options are the same. So seek out the look and model designation that appeals to you. This is a 1998 Formula with the optional removable glass roof panels. *Pontiac*

A 1998 Trans Am. Like the Camaro, the TA got a nose, tail, side panel, and wheel redesign to go with the new 305-horse LS1 engines and other drivetrain upgrades. This car is a non-WS6 model with the optional removable glass roof panels. *Pontiac*

be outdone by the SS, Pontiac also went back into its history for a performance nameplate that could inspire a special model.

In the Firebird's case, it was called "Ram Air," after Pontiac's legendary 400-ci Ram Air III and Ram Air IV V-8s of the 1960s and early 1970s. Pontiac initially went to Street Legal Performance (SLP), a Detroit-based performance house, to develop a Ram Air Firebird model much in the vein of the Camaro SS. That wasn't much of a stretch, as SLP was already building its own quasi-factory performance model called the Firebird Firehawk.

The Ram Air was first introduced in 1997, and included a special fiberglass hood incorporating a cold-air intake system. Other changes were larger wheels and special Ram Air identification. Horsepower was also an SS-like 305. Pontiac took Ram Air development and production in-house for 1998, and like the 1998 Chevy SS, horsepower was further upped to 320. We've not explored them in any great detail, as these limited production models are still well in excess of our $20,000 ceiling and are likely to

be for some time. The same can be said of the blue-and-white-only 1999 30th Anniversary edition Trans-Am. The SLP Firehawk is a bit of a quandary; though the Firehawk program had a certain factory recognition in that the cars could be ordered through Pontiac dealers, and the cars did offer marginally enhanced performance over the standard Firebirds, they were not a pure, factory special edition. Nothing wrong with that, but owners often try to command a substantial price premium for Firehawks, and there isn't enough substance or "factory authorized, limited production" value to justify it.

Reliability-wise, anything we said about the Camaro holds true for the Firebird as well, so we'll refer you back to Chapter 6. While neither wins awards for rear-seat room, cargo capacity, visibility, or materials quality, these cars drip testosterone from every pore. They're not exactly subtle, but from a horsepower-per-dollar standpoint, they are an outstanding buy, especially if you can find a V-8, six-speed model in a handsome color combination that hasn't been abused.

Although this 1998 Trans Am convertible isn't under the $20K limit just yet, slightly earlier Trans Am and Formula models are. There's little functional difference between the two; most of it relates to appearance and some option availability. *Pontiac*

The Trans Am, Formula, and Camaro Z28's Corvette-derived, all-aluminum-LS1-derived V-8 is nothing to look at with its valve-cover-mounted coil packs, black plastic intake manifold, and plethora of tubes and wires. But it matters little, for this is one of the best performance engines ever made. It's tough, torquey, inexpensive, easy to modify, and meets the same emission requirements as do small four bangers. Looks good to us. *Pontiac*

SPECIFICATIONS (1994 FIREBIRD FORMULA)

Body style. . . . . Two door, four passenger
Drivetrain layout . . . . Front engine, rear drive
Engine type . . . . OHV V-8
Displacement, liter/cc 5.7/5,733
Horsepower, hp @ rpm . . . . SAE net 275 @ 5,000
Torque, ft-lb @ rpm . . . . SAE net 325 @ 2,400
Transmission . . . . 6-speed manual
Wheelbase, in. 101.1
Length, in. 195.6
Width, in.. . . . . 74.5
Height, in. 52.0
Base curb weight, lb 3,425
Suspension, f/r . . . . Upper and lower A-arms/live axle
Steering type. . . . . Rack and pinion
Brakes, f/r . . . . Disc/disc

PERFORMANCE

Acceleration, 0–60 mph . . . . 6.0 sec.
Standing quarter
mile, sec/mph 14.4/98.0
Source . . . . Road & Track

TYPICAL PARTS/REPAIR PRICES

Major tune-up/service. $700
Air filter 10
Shock absorber 101
Catalytic converter(s) 108
Clutch replacement 1,200

WEBSITES

firebirdtaclub.com

REPORT CARD

Engine	A-
Transmission	A-
Power/Weight Ratio	B+
Handling	A
Braking	A
Ride	B+
Exterior Styling	B+
Interior Styling	B+
Interior Function	B+
Cargo Capacity	C-
Everyday Usability	B-
Reliability	B+
Fit and Finish	A
Market Availability	C+
Resale Value Potential	B
Fun Factor	A-
Bang for Buck	C+
Aftermarket Interest	B+
Club Support	A

Porsche 944 S2 (1990–1991), 968 (1992–1995)

There's no question that Porsche is one of the great names in sports car history. But they've certainly become expensive: a reasonably well-equipped Boxster is a $40K+ proposition. But with a little shopping, and a little luck, it's possible to "join the club" within the outer price limit of this book.

Porsche's last 944 model, the S2, and the 968, which some consider to be yet the final variation on the 944 theme, trace their heritage back to the original water-cooled, front-engined Porsche 924 that debuted in the U. S. market in 1976. Porsche is known for launching a platform, sticking with it, and continuously bettering it over time. And that was the case here; while it's not worth tracking the 15 years-worth of model evolution that led up to the 944 S2 models of 1990 and 1991, suffice it to say that this was a highly developed car by that time.

The 944 had been around since 1983, but Porsche continually updated and upgraded it to keep it relatively fresh in the marketplace. Its 3.0 liter-engine is considered positively huge for a modern day four-cylinder, but precision machining and assembly, plus the use of balance shafts, make it amazingly smooth. The power levels and that smoothness will fool most into thinking it's a six. *Porsche Cars North America*

The previously offered, naturally aspirated and turbo 944 models both went away in favor of a single, 3.0-liter non-turbo four-cylinder-powered version. This large, high-tech powerplant featured double-overhead cams, four valves per cylinder, and twin counter-rotating balance shafts to counteract the potential for vibration in such a large inline four. It was all quite effective: an impressive 208 horsepower, with smoothness that rivaled some six-cylinder engines. There's not another naturally aspirated four listed in this book packing this much power—with the exception of the 968. Only one transmission was offered, a five-speed manual transaxle mounted in the rear of the car for better weight balance.

The 944 has always been noted as an exceptional handler. Its MacPherson strut front and torsion bar rear suspension is straightforward yet exceptionally well tuned, and Porsche's rack-and-pinion steering offers feel that's second to none. The four-wheel vented disc brakes with standard ABS are excellent, and there's a lot to be said for the 944's rear drive and low center of gravity; its hard to fault a late-model Porsche when it comes to excellent driving dynamics.

Up until 1990, all previous 944s were 2+2 hatchbacks. But that changed with the introduction of the 944 S2 Cabriolet. The large rear bubble-like rear window gave way to a conventional trunk, and the Cab also sported a power convertible top. Importantly, Porsche sufficiently reinforced the chassis to compensate for the reduction in structural rigidity lost to the lack of roof structure.

The 944 S2 coupe cost more than $40,000 by this time (the original 924 cost about a third of that), but at least it was well equipped: cruise control, air

From the rear, the 944 S2 looks a lot more like the original mid-1970s 944 on which it was based. That rear-under tray isn't for looks, however; it's a functional aerodynamic spoiler, which along with the upper wing, really helps the 944's tail stay planted at speed. *Porsche Cars North America*

conditioning, fog lights, dual air bags, power windows/mirrors/locks, electric sunroof (coupe), alarm system, and alloy wheels came standard. Desirable extras are a leather-trimmed interior and a sport suspension. The 1991 S2 was essentially a carryover, but did incorporate a few subtle body updates and a revised rear spoiler.

By the 1992 model year, the 944 had been around nearly a decade. But the Boxster was yet to be a glimmer in Stuttgart's eye, and an "entry level" Porsche model was still necessary, so it was time for a more substantive update of the 944. Along with it came a new chassis designation, 968. This was appropriate, as Porsche claimed nearly 80 percent of the car was new or redesigned.

Porsche needed to keep an "entry model" (a relative term, in the case of Porsche) in its lineup, yet the Boxster was still years away. What to do? Give the 944 yet one more revamp. New front and rear fascias and fenders really broke away the 968 from the look of its 924/944 predecessors, including 928-style headlights and Carrera-style wheels. The new six-speed was a plus too. *Porsche Cars North America*

The 968 received new sheet-metal front and rear; only the door stampings were identical to the 944's. The most visible change was the integration of the open headlights into new sheet metal that looked somewhat like both the larger, V-8-powered 928 and the standard bearer of the Porsche lineup, the 911. The suspension system was also carried over largely intact, save for stiffer shocks, springs, and bushings in the name of increased handling prowess.

The S2's 3.0-liter four remained, but was treated to Porsche's newly developed VarioCam system; its variable valve timing technology increased the engine's horsepower rating to an even more impressive 236. Transmission offerings were further upgraded, offering the 968 buyer a choice of a new six-speed manual, or a four-speed Tiptronic automatic with sequential shift capability. The interior design was largely a carryover, though cabin enhancements included an automatic climate control system. The 968 continued to be available in both coupe and Cabriolet body styles.

As impressive as the 944 S2 was, the 968 just went a bit further in most every dimension: the look was fresher (if not all new), and who wouldn't welcome the flexibility of more power and transmission choices. A popular option for those seeking maximum performance is the P30 sport suspension package, which includes adjustable gas shocks and larger front brakes; this is best when combined with the also optional 17-inch rolling stock.

Nineteen ninety-three was a carryover year, and changes for 1994 were minimal: new wheel and seat designs, plus a bit of fabric and color shuffling. In mid-1994, Porsche also began offering a Torsen limited-slip rear differential for better traction during cornering. 1995 turned out to be the 968's final year in production, but for serious drivers, it may be the best, as Porsche reshuffled the componentry for the sport suspension package (now called option P31) for even bet-

Here's another one you won't find within our price guidelines, the 968 Club Sport. But this photo gives a good look at the tail end of the 968 and how much it differed from the previous 944. *Porsche Cars North America*

Don't expect to find a 968 Cab for less than $20K anytime soon, but it could happen as the model is now out of production, and most "cost-conscious" Porsche owners are trading up to Boxsters. The top stack is not particularly neat, but then again, the 968 was never originally intended to be bodied as a convertible. *Porsche Cars North America*

ter handling. Shocks, springs, and brakes all were upgraded, and the 17-inch wheels and tires were now a standard part of the package. Porsche also offered a lighter weight "club racer" model called the 968 CS in 1993, though these are rare, and not likely to be found below our $20,000 price limit.

After so many years on the market, and many hardware updates, you'd expect the 9544/968 to be well-developed, reliable cars. And they are, if well cared for. The thing to remember with a Porsche, however, is that the cost of parts and service is near, or at, the top of the range for most of the cars we discuss in this book. Things don't break often, but when they do, be prepared to pay for the repairs. Periodic care is limited to oil and filter changes, plus an oil change for the manual transaxle every 15,000 miles or so.

The big maintenance issue on S2/968s is the care and feeding of the camshaft drive chain—the mechanical link between the two camshafts. The built-in tensioner that keeps it adjusted ultimately wears out, as does the chain itself. If the chain brakes, pistons and valves could come in contact, destroying the upper half of the engine—that is, big bucks. Have the chain and tensioner checked every 20,000–25,000 miles by someone who knows late-model Porsches, and replace either as required, when needed. The manual transmission and clutch are tough components, and should go 100,000 miles before they need attention. Earlier 944s suffered frequent water pump failures, but that doesn't seem to be a problem on these later S2 engines. Steering racks are usually shot by 100,000 miles, and even rebuilt units are upwards of $1,000.

It is hard to recommend a Tiptronic-equipped 968 over a six-speed: besides being out of character for a true sports car, this "clutchless manual" technology was somewhat in its infancy, and the transmission is a bit slow to respond to shift commands. The unit is reliable, just not all that fun. Stick with the stick. It's also worth mentioning that many 968 models, particularly the later Cabs, aren't yet available for less than our $20K ceiling, but the cars are new enough that a bit more depreciation is still likely; from then on, they should be obtainable and hold their value given good care.

The original 924 and early 944s suffered from a reputation as not being "real Porsches." While 911-ophiles will always criticize any car with a front-mounted engine and water cooling, the 944/968 seems to suffer less of that. No matter what the clubbies say, these later cars represent a way to get into a Porsche that makes a great everyday driver, carry modern hardware (like ABS brakes and air bags), offer exceptional handling and a 50/50 weight balance, and are reasonably affordable in the process.

SPECIFICATIONS (1990 944 S2)

Body style	Two door, four passenger
Drivetrain layout	Front engine, rear drive
Engine type	DOHC I-4
Displacement, liter/cc	3.0/2,990
Horsepower, hp @ rpm	SAE net 208 @ 5,800
Torque, ft-lb @ rpm	SAE net 207 @ 4,100
Transmission	6-speed manual
Wheelbase, in.	94.5
Length, in.	168.9
Width, in.	68.3
Height, in.	50.2
Base curb weight, lb	2,985
Suspension, f/r	MacPherson strut/semi-trailing arm
Steering type	Rack and pinion
Brakes, f/r	Disc/disc

PERFORMANCE

Acceleration, 0–60 mph	6.7 sec.
Standing quarter mile, sec/mph	14.7
Source	Road & Track

TYPICAL PARTS/REPAIR PRICES

Major tune-up/service	$950
Air filter	13
Shock absorber	140
Catalytic converter(s)	127
Clutch replacement	1,400

WEBSITES

pca.com
porscheclub.com

REPORT CARD

Engine	B+
Transmission	B+
Power/Weight Ratio	B+
Handling	A-
Braking	B+
Ride	B
Exterior Styling	A-
Interior Styling	A-
Interior Function	B+
Cargo Capacity	C+
Everyday Usability	B-
Reliability	B+
Fit and Finsh	A-
Market Availability	B-
Resale Value Potential	B
Fun Factor	A-
Bang for Buck	B
Aftermarket Interest	B
Club Support	A-

Toyota MR2
(1991–1995)

Toyota had a tough time with sports cars in the 1990s. It's not that they weren't good cars—in fact, both the second-generation MR2 and the latest version Toyota Supra (see Chapter 26) were in fact exceptionally interesting machines. But they were both getting a reputation for being overpriced when they were new, and closed sporting coupes were about to be replaced by a raft of new roadsters and convertibles beginning about the time these two went away. So who knows? Now, both enjoy a loyal following and are perhaps becoming more recognized for the well-built and fun-to-drive cars they are.

Most race cars have their engines placed amidships for good reasons, primarily centered weight distribution and the potential for a lower polar moment of inertia—both thought of as design elements that create a great-handling car. Yet midengined street cars have usually come from the designer labels: Ferrari, Lamborghini, etc. The Porsche 914 and Fiat X1/9 of the early 1970s bucked that trend, and so did the first-generation MR2

This cutaway drawing of the 1991 MR2 Turbo shows the exotic midengine design, MacPherson strut four-wheel independent suspension, and intimate cockpit. David Kimball cutaway, *Toyota*

Toyota or slightly pre-shrunk Ferrari 308 GTS? The similarity is undeniable. This is the 1993 MR2 Turbo. *Toyota*

of 1985–1989. It was a knife-edged, close-coupled little runabout, both in terms of handling and its Origami-inspired, crisply folded body styling. When it came time for a redo, Toyota made it a bit larger and a lot more stylish.

Often called a "baby-Ferrari," the "Mk2" (not an official Toyota designation) MR2 was a smooth looker when it appeared in the United States as a 1991 model, and its styling has held up very well today. The only

touch that might date it a bit is the use of pop-up headlights, when most cars have gone to large, faired-in glass-covered bulbs, but many people still like them, and again they certainly contribute to the MR2's smooth look. This new-gen MR also packed a lot of equipment not even offered on the original, such as optional power steering, available anti-lock brakes, and a driver-side air bag (dual air bags came along with the 1994 model).

Probably the ultimate second-generation MR2: a closed-roof, 1995 Turbo. Note later, larger wheel design. Even though this car had ultimately priced itself out of the market, the midengine layout lives on in today's MR2 Spyder. *Toyota*

This shot highlights the MR2's exotic lines and the removable roof section, a la Corvette. While Toyota made the effort to reinforce the MR's platform to make up for the loss in structural rigidity due to the missing roof, it's still not quite as solid as the fully closed version. Still, it may be a worthy trade-off to you if the sports car experience must include the proverbial wind in your hair. *Toyota*

Two models were available: the standard MR2, powered by a 2.2-liter 130-horsepower inline-four, and the MR2 Turbo, packing heat in the form of a turbocharged, 2.0-liter four cranking out a more-than-respectable 200 horsepower at 6,000 rpm. Each were borrowed and developed from various versions of the Celica. Although the Turbo is obviously the hottest MR2, the base-engined model is nothing to sneeze at. The standard four is a cast-iron block/alloy head unit, with double-overhead camshafts and four valves per cylinder. While it doesn't offer some of the higher tech goodies that showed up in the latter half of the 1990s, such as variable valve timing, remember that the MR2 is a bit lighter than many larger coupes and sedans, so it offers a reasonable power-to-weight ratio even in standard form. The naturally aspirated MR could be had with either a five-speed manual transmission or an electronically managed four-speed automatic. The latter was never a particularly sporty combo, so we recommend the stick.

Performance mongers will automatically seek out the Turbo. This 2.0-liter engine also boasts cast-iron block/aluminum-head construction, 16 valves, and DOHC, plus an intercooler, which we feel is a must for any turbocharged application. An intercooler cools down the intake air, which makes more horsepower and protects against detonation—any engine's least favorite acquaintance. The turbo is also a relatively torquey piece for its size, serving up a maximum 200 ft-lb at 3,200 rpm. There's only one tranny available, a five-speed manual.

As noted, MR2s weren't cheap (in fact, the last of the rare 1995 Turbos ran nearly 30 grand!) but they did offer a high feature content. The midengine layout dictates an all-independent suspension system, and there was no skimping on brake hardware either: four-wheel vented disc brakes with optional ABS. Power-assist for the quick-ratio rack-and-pinion steering was provided via an electric motor, decreasing the system's parasitic power drain on the engine. The amount of assist varied with engine speed and cornering conditions; you got high boost during parking, and more steering feel while cutting the corners.

Both the naturally aspirated MR and the Turbo could be had in closed coupe form or with a "T-Bar" roof. This Targa-typeglass panel could be removed to let some air in—not unlike that of a Ferrari 308 GTS, again with which the MR2 is often compared. A more conventional, pop-up sunroof was also available, with leather seats and one of several high-zoot stereo systems being optional.

Nineteen ninety-two was essentially a carryover year, but there were substantive changes for 1993. Midengined cars are noted for a handling attitude called oversteer, meaning a tendency for the rear end to want to come around or spin during a corner. The skilled driver usually enjoys a car that can be provoked into oversteer, but if the car does it too quickly, or can't be reeled-in in time, well, let's say the result can be expensive. MR2s for 1991–1992 were noted for too much oversteer at the handling limit, though again, this shouldn't be construed to mean they are unsafe. So Toyota took steps to control this condition, namely a switch to larger (better-looking) 15-inch rolling stock,

24-5 The MR2 Turbo's power output is virtually identical to that found in Toyota's Celica All-Trac Turbo. The All-Trac is a much heavier car, however, so the MR2 handily wins the power-to-weight-ratio contest against its heavier stablemate. The MR2 is often referred to as a "baby Ferrari 308," and its 200-horsepower rating is just about the same as the earliest, fuel-injected, two-valve/cylinder 308's was. Had Ferrari been building this early-1980s model at the same time the MR2 Turbo was on the market, the Toyota would have actually been faster! *Toyota*

stiffer springs and shocks at all four corners, revised suspension bushings, and lower links. The result was a much more neutral handling attitude.

The already-adequate brakes benefited from larger rotors front and rear, and a crisper, shorter-throw shifter linkage also improved the driving experience. Base prices continued to increase, but so did standard equipment levels: Turbos now carried a cruise control, power windows and locks, a power antenna, and an upgraded stereo system as standard. The improved 1993s (which actually started showing up in the marketplace in mid-1992) also sported a larger front air intake and body-colored mirrors.

Given all the changes for 1993, 1994 was pretty much a carryover model; physical changes were limited to a new rear fascia, redesigned taillights, a new standard single piece rear spoiler, and a bit more body-colored trim. The suspension received even further tuning, though it was much less substantive than before: re-valved shocks and revised alignment specs. 1995, the final year the MR2 was offered in the United States, saw only a bit of equipment shuffling for the base model, and the Turbo was discontinued in a few markets. 1995 closed the book on the MR nameplate—until the new, midengined MR2 Spyder came along for 2000.

The MR2 is a midengined sports car, yes, but a reasonably refined one. You sit low, there's room for only you and a guest, there's minimum luggage space, but who cares? It's a great car for the mountain roads in your area. Having owned DeTomaso Panteras in my past, I enjoy the handling aspects of a midengine car (they tend to pivot in the middle, rather than on the front axle, during hard cornering). The MR has reasonably quick reflexes, and offers satisfactory handling feedback for a car saddled with MacPherson strut suspension front and rear. Turbos will haul 0–60 in around six seconds, and at 200 horsepower, its output is as good as any VR6 or VTEC motor you'll find in today's new cars. As noted, the naturally aspirated base model offers reasonable driving fun and a lot of style for the money, but the performance-oriented driver will head straight for the Turbo.

The T-top option is nice but does reduce the chassis structural integrity, so if handling is high on your list, we'd recommend sticking to the coupe, or perhaps one with the sunroof if you need some air. Another thing going for you is Toyota's reputation for high-quality materials, good fit and finish, plus solid reliability. Parts, however, are not cheap, so an MR2 is another car where it really pays to find a well-cared-for example.

While there's no reason to run away from a well-maintained, low-mileage, primo condition 1991–1992 MR2, the much-improved 1993–1995 is clearly the model of choice; 1995s are exceptionally rare, with probably less than 500 being sold before Toyota turned off the tap. They handle better, have higher levels of standard equipment, and look better in their more monochromatic trim and on their larger wheels and tires. Even at that, the five-spoke alloys are a bit bland, and a set of premium, aftermarket 16 inchers really spices up the car's look (and further sharpens its steering response too).

As noted, MR2s are well-built cars, but there are a few things to make sure of. As with just about any car, evidence of regular engine oil and filter changes is important, but "important" becomes "critical" when it comes to a Turbo. Turbochargers use the engine's oil supply for lubrication, and cruddy oil can cause the turbo's main bearings to head south. If your MR2's turbo is shot (the telltale signs are sluggish acceleration without that usual turbo pull from about 3,000 rpm and above and/or a whining turbocharger bearing), figure at least $1,000 for a rebuilt unit, plus labor, right off the bat.

A bit of black, sooty buildup in the exhaust pipes is also somewhat common, and may indicate the need for repair or replacement of the oxygen sensor or one of several other engine control system sensors—or at least the need for a tune-up and system adjustment. Also check around the turbo for oil leaks. The rubber seals around the T-bar roof deteriorate, and can allow water leakage and/or wind noise. The MR2's vented disc rotors are expensive, so any that are warped or deeply grooved will mean an expensive brake job and perhaps some price negotiation. And the MR2 requires wheel alignments both front and rear, so see that this is done before replacing worn tires.

Handsome, rare, reasonably sophisticated, reliable (even if a bit expensive to care for), and boasting an exotic midengine layout, the MR2 is a different-from-the-rest sports car you can happily drive every day.

SPECIFICATIONS (1995 MR2 TURBO)

Body style . . . . Two door, two passenger
Drivetrain layout . . . . Midengine, rear drive
Engine type . . . . Turbocharged DOHC I-4
Displacement, liter/cc 2.0/1,998
Horsepower, hp @ rpm . . . . SAE net 200 @ 6,000
Torque, ft-lb @ rpm . . . . SAE net 200 @ 3,200
Transmission . . . . 5-speed manual
Wheelbase, in. 94.5
Length, in. 164.2
Width, in. 66.9
Height, in. 48.6
Base curb weight, lb 2,888
Suspension, f/r . . . . MacPherson strut/Chapman strut
Steering type. . . . . Rack and pinion
Brakes, f/r . . . . Disc/disc

PERFORMANCE

Acceleration, 0–60 mph . . . . 7.1 sec.
Standing quarter
mile, sec/mph 15.4
Source. . . . . Road & Track

TYPICAL PARTS/REPAIR PRICES

Major tune-up/service. $250
Air filter 10
Shock absorber 101
Catalytic converter(s) 87
Clutch replacement 790

WEBSITE

mr2.com

Toyota Celica All-Trac Turbo (1990–1993)

REPORT CARD

Engine	A-
Transmission	A-
Power/Weight Ratio	A-
Handling	A-
Braking	B+
Ride	B
Exterior Styling	B
Interior Styling	B
Interior Function	B
Cargo Capacity	B
Everyday Usability	B
Reliability	B
Fit and Finsh	B+
Market Availability	D
Resale Value Potential	B+
Fun Factor	B
Bang for Buck	C
Aftermarket Interest	C
Club Support	C

Much like the previously discussed BMW M3, the Celica All-Trac Turbo (which we'll refer to as the All-Trac) is another one of those rare birds that was used to homologate a certain body style and power-train configuration for racing. In this case, the All-Trac came to market to certify the use of a turbocharged, all-wheel-drive Celica for international rally competition. The All-Trac was expensive when it was new, not many were sold, and there are special maintenance issues to be mindful of—but its rarity and performance cache make it desirable to drivers who want something different. Think of it as a sort of Japanese Audi quattro.

Toyota introduced the All-Trac in 1988, on the fourth-generation Celica platform. Its main calling cards were a 2.0-liter 190-horsepower turbocharged, intercooled four-cylinder engine; full-time all-wheel-drive, four-wheel disc brakes and optional ABS, which was not at all common on Japanese (or any) compact cars in 1988. The interior received all the trappings that Toyota offered at the time, and the outside got special fascias, rocker panels, a rear spoiler, and front fog lights. It's sub-eight-second 0–60 time was impressive, as was its

Toyota did little to distinguish the All-Trac Turbo from more plebeian Celicas, but that may be part of its appeal—a genuine sleeper. Even the rear wing was the same one as found on the Celica GT. *Toyota*

The hood is one of the few pieces that does identify an All-Trac: Note the central hood scoop and louver-style gills. No convertible or notchback All-Tracs were ever offered, with the hatchback being the single body style. This is a 1992 model. *Toyota*

$20,000–23,000 price range, remembering that a 2001 Toyota MR2 Spyder cost about the same, more than a dozen years later.

The Celica was given a substantive redo for 1990; the All-Trac model, which was sold for all four of the fifth-gen Celica's model years, remained the lineup's top performer. The All-Trac was offered only in the hatchback body style, interesting as closed coupes generally have stiffer chassis structures, and might have been a more natural pick for the performance version. But hatches were seen as the upmarket model, so it probably made the most sense at the time.

The All-Trac engine remained at 2.0 liters, but a slight reconfiguration to the exhaust system and engine management software made for a 10-horsepower boost. That meant an even 200 horsepower and an equal 200 ft-lb of torque. That scoop atop the hood is functional, drawing air into the liquid-to-air intercooler. Use of an intercooler is important in a turbo installation, as this radiator-like device cools the intake charge for not only more power but reduced threat of pre-ignition ("pinging"), which can dramatically shorten the life of a turbocharged engine. The only transmission offering was a five-speed manual.

The full-time all-wheel-drive system was designed to increase traction and cornering grip, and that it did effectively. Its main component is a viscous coupling center differential that orchestrates power front-to-back depending on the axle that's getting the best traction. It's all quite transparent to the driver, as there are no controls or switches needed to manage the system. Also required, of course, were an additional differential and set of axles at the rear, as the standard Celica was front-wheel drive.

As noted, the All-Trac came standard with most every option Toyota had in the book: power steering, windows, and locks, an upgraded sound system, and the like. There were few options, the main ones being the aforementioned ABS system, leather-trimmed seats, and beginning in 1990, an absolutely impressive System 10 Audio package with 10 speakers, 220 watts of power, graphic equalizer, and one component that was still somewhat rare back then—a CD player. One other unusual feature found only on the All-Trac was a tilt-away steering wheel, which automatically tilted up to ease entry and exit.

Toyota hit most of the All-Trac's front-end lighting in one way or another. The headlights are of course pop-up units, the driving lights are seen behind the lower fascia's horizontal bars, and even the upper turn signals are worked into the black plastic upper-grille band. Note the aerodynamic mirrors. *Toyota*

Were it not for the badging and slightly more aggressive rear-wing and lower-rear fascia, you wouldn't know an All-Trac from a base-model Celica. Now for some, that might be seen as a disadvantage; you want people to know you have something special. But for others, the All-Trac ranks high as a "sleeper." The Celica's overall shape still look good, but a more modern set of rally-inspired alloy wheels would really wake up its styling. *Toyota*

The intercooler is mounted high in the engine bay, and its intake surface mates directly to the functional hood scoop. An intercooler is an important component on a turbocharged engine, as the cooler intake air not only makes more horsepower, but prevents detonation ("pinging") under high boost load. It's a robust powerplant, but not cheap to repair if it incurs major damage, so check those service records carefully. Toyota also took a cue from the aftermarket: note the structural braces that triangulate the shock towers to the firewall. *Toyota*

All All-Tracs translated to impressive performance. As with the earlier versions, 0-60 times were regularly in the 7.5–7.9-second range, depending on who was doing the testing. It would have even been faster, had it not been for the All-Trac's somewhat porky 3,300-pound weight—all the extra hardware adds up to extra pounds. And it certainly gripped well too; skid pad g-ratings of .86–.88 are good now, and great then. With modern rubber on wider 16-inch wheels, and perhaps some shock/sway bar tuning, .9g or better should be within easy reach.

Nineteen ninety-one was a carryover year, save for the usual few new colors. The same went for 1992, from a mechanical standpoint, though the front fascia and rear taillight clusters were mildly redesigned. The Celica was remodeled into its sixth iteration for 1994—but the All-Trac didn't make the U.S. lineup. It was getting expensive—well over $25,000—and that seemed like a lot for a Celica. Although Toyota enjoyed great success on the international rally circuit with it for the past six years, given the relatively unknown status of rallying in this country and the All-Trac's low sales volumes, re-certifying it for the new body style just didn't make sense. Plus an all-new, twin-turbo Supra was coming for 1994, ready to take its place as the performance flagship in the lineup.

Given the complexity (translation: expense) of systems such as the turbocharged engine and all-wheel-drive system, it's paramount to focus on condition and maintenance when contemplating an All-Trac. Be willing to pay extra for a low-mileage, well-cared-for example with a solid maintenance history; an All-Trac with a whining turbo and clunking center is good reason to run. Religious oil changes are critical.

The All-Trac's increased cornering grip capability also means suspension components (bushings, shock absorbers, wheel bearings) tended to wear out more quickly. The rear differential mount wears easily but is not an expensive repair. As you'd expect, clutches take their share of abuse, and any car with more than 75,000 miles on it will need one, if it hasn't been replaced already.

All-Tracs are well engineered, well built, and reliable; not at all finicky. But their high-performance nature, complex systems, and rarity mean that when something is broken or worn out, there are few cheap fixes. Most parts are still available from Toyota, and there is the usual club/Internet network to help with advice. And given good care, they tend to hold their value.

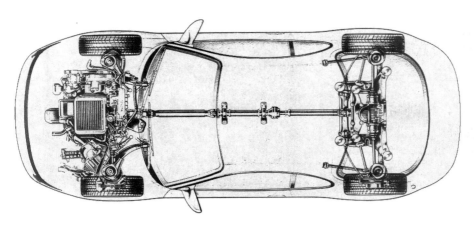

This diagram shows off the All-Trac's sophisticated driveline. The rear suspension is fully independent, and the all-important viscous-coupling center differential is seen between the two driveshafts. These diff units have proven to be extremely tough, and can take a lot more horsepower should you wish to modify the engine. *Toyota*

SPECIFICATIONS (1990 CELICA ALL-TRAC TURBO)

Body style . . . . Two door, two passenger
Drivetrain layout . . . . Front engine, all-wheel-drive
Engine type . . . . Turbocharged DOHC I-4
Displacement, liter/cc 2.0/1,998
Horsepower, hp @ rpm . . . . SAE net 200 @ 6,000
Torque, ft-lb @ rpm . . . . SAE net 200 @ 3,200
Transmission . . . . 5-speed manual
Wheelbase, in. 99.4
Length, in. 174.0
Width, in. 68.7
Height, in. 50.4
Base curb weight, lb 3,270
Suspension, f/r . . . . MacPherson strut/Chapman strut
Steering type. . . . . Rack and pinion
Brakes, f/r . . . . Disc/disc

PERFORMANCE

Acceleration, 0–60 mph . . . . 7.5 sec.
Standing quarter
mile, sec/mph 15.7/87.2
Source . . . . Road & Track

TYPICAL PARTS/REPAIR PRICES

Major tune-up/service. $295
Air filter 10
Shock absorber 43
Catalytic converter(s) 140
Clutch replacement 1,050

WEBSITE

geocities.com/MotorCity/Downs/3419

Chapter 26

Toyota Supra (1993-1/2–1998)

FOR
- Sophisticated powertrain
- Wild looks
- Great long distance cruiser

AGAINST
- Cramped rear quarters
- Not everyone loves the wild looks
- Model availability is spotty

HOT PICK
Any year Turbo six-speed

REPORT CARD

Engine	A
Transmission	A
Power/Weight Ratio	B+
Handling	A-
Braking	A-
Ride	A
Exterior Styling	A
Interior Styling	B+
Interior Function	B+
Cargo Capacity	B+
Everyday Usability	B+
Reliability	A-
Fit and Finish	A
Market Availability	B-
Resale Value Potential	B
Fun Factor	A-
Bang for Buck	B-
Aftermarket Interest	A-
Club Support	A-

At the time of its mid-1993 introduction, more than one enthusiast magazine called the fourth-generation Toyota Supra Turbo "a Japanese Ferrari." And why not: it has swoopy bodywork, 320 horsepower, a six-speed manual transmission, and a chassis rigged for serious handling. Heck, the Ferrari 348 of the day was only good for 300 horse, and cost about twice as much.

The previous-generation Supra was a nice car but was criticized as becoming a bit of a "lounge lizard": it was heavy, didn't accelerate or handle all that well for a supposed GT, and seemed to be more focused on electronic features than real performance. Toyota went the "hard core" route in developing the "Mk. IV" Supra, and though it was still a largish 2+2 (as opposed to a lithe two-seater like the Mazda RX-7), the transformation was considerable. The Supra went on a diet and came out several hundred pounds lighter than the old car. The curvaceous

Don't mistake the Supra for a compact; it's actually quite a large car and sits well on its 17-inch rolling stock. It was also one of the first cars to employ flush-glass, multi-element headlamp clusters when it appeared in mid-1993. *Toyota*

The 1995 model was virtually identical to the year before. The Supra did the aftermarket one better, by offering what was, at that time, one of the most outrageous rear wing designs ever factory-offered. *Toyota*

shape was a wind tunnel trimmed to manage air at high speed. And the powertrains were all new. Besides the choice of naturally aspirated or Turbo models, Toyota offered the Supra in standard coupe and "Sport Roof" body styles; the Sport Roof has a Porsche Targa-like removable roof panel.

Toyota developed a twin-turbo variant of its DOHC 3.0-liter twin cam inline six that uses a sequential boost management system not unlike that found in the Mazda RX-7. With a sequentially managed twin-turbo setup, the engine runs on one turbo at low rpm, with the second phasing in the middle rpm ranges for mid-high rpm power. Needless to say, it takes some

sophisticated electronics to manage this process, but it works quite well in the Supra; the phasing in of the second, slightly larger, turbo is barely detectable. The system also benefits from an intercooler, which helps cool the intake charge for better performance and lower risk of detonation. The Turbo was available with a six-speed manual transmission or a four-speed automatic, though as we'll see later, various combinations came and went over the car's production life. Supra Turbos also employ a Torsen limited-slip rear differential to help get all that grunt to the ground.

The Supra Turbo also had the underpinnings to match the punch. A well-tuned, fully independent sus-

One unusual styling element is that the Supra's gaping mouth is grilleless, as clearly seen on this 1994 Turbo. All sorts of hardware is visible, including the intercooler. The Supra was also one of the first production cars to make use of multi-element headlights. *David Newhardt*

By the time of this 1997 Anniversary model, details had changed, but the overall car remained much the same. Note little details like the use of clear glass for the headlight housings, clear and amber—as opposed to solid amber turn-signal lenses and chrome wheels. This car also has the removable roof panel. *Toyota*

The cockpit resembles that of Mazda RX-7, only on a larger scale. The Nakamichi stereo sounds amazing, even against some of today's best systems, and the six-speed stick's short, direct linkage is a joy to use. *Toyota*

The Supra Turbo was often hailed as "a Japanese Ferrari at half the price." That's a compliment to the Toyota, but in truth, the Supra Turbo would actually outperform the Ferrari 328 GTS it's so casually parked next to. *David Newhardt*

pension and 17-inch performance-rated rolling stock help deliver impressive stick: *Motor Trend* achieved a Viper-like .98g on its skidpad, better than just about anything in this book, again depending on whose numbers you're comparing. The vented, four-wheel disc brakes are equipped with four-channel ABS as standard, and again deliver stopping distances that are up there with any other car we've discussed (*Motor Trend*'s 60-0 miles per hour brake test distance was just 109 feet).

Not to be outdone, the naturally aspirated Supra is an impressive performer in its own right. It uses a non-turbo 3.0-liter six, rated at 220 horsepower—remember, the V-8-powered Mustang GT of the day was only good for 225. The standard Supra comes with a choice of a five-speed manual or four-speed automatic, and could also be had in standard coupe or Sport Roof form.

The Supra's cabin is elegantly styled and all business. The dash is a driver-oriented, wraparound affair that puts all controls within easy reach, and including a large tach front and center. Supras have cloth/vinyl-upholstered seats, though most Turbos came with the optional leather trim. These chairs are comfortable and nicely bolstered, though rear seat room is fair at best; think of the Supra as a big 2+2, rather than a four-adults coupe. The large rear deck opens to reveal a larger-than-average cargo hold. Air conditioning, power windows/locks/mirrors, and dual front air bags are standard.

By now, you've gathered that the Turbo is fast and handles well, but that speed and cornering prowess didn't come at the expense of a buckboard ride or a noisy cabin. The ride quality is firm and well controlled, yet somehow remains supple and smooth. There's very little wind noise or road rumble. The clutch is light and progressive, the six-speed shifter offers short throws and a crisp linkage. Supra's variable ratio rack-and-pinion steering is a little on the light side; there's adequate road feel, but it's still a little over-boosted. And the engine sounds wonderful: a deep burble that increases to a silken wail, as only a straight six can deliver, overlaid with the rise and fall of the whirring turbos.

The Supra lived a somewhat star-crossed life during its production run: even though it's an amazing performer, it was expensive for the day, and sold in relatively small numbers—though these factors may make it all the more desirable now. Various engine/transmission/body style configurations came and went over 5-1/2 model years, best illustrated by this chart:

	1993	1994	1995	1996	1997	1998
Turbo, 6-speed, coupe	•	•	•			
Turbo, 6-speed, Sport Roof	•	•	•		•	•
Turbo, auto, Sport Roof	•	•	•	•	•	•
Supra, 5-speed, Sport Roof	•	•	•	•	•	
Supra, auto, Sport Roof	•	•	•	•	•	•
Supra, auto, coupe	•	•	•	•	•	•
Supra, 5-speed, coupe	•	•	•	•	•	

Source: www.mkIV.com

After its mid-1993 intro, the 1994 and 1995 Supras were largely unchanged. For 1996, there was one new color, the addition of a fabric-covered rear seat, a fully manual cloth-covered driver seat, and the deletion of heating elements in the outside mirrors on no-turbo coupe models. But the bigger news was the deletion of the top-performing Turbo/six-speed combination, due to "ever-increasing emission requirements," according to Toyota. That's a dubious statement at best, because it was back for 1997!

For 1997, the Supra's 15th year on the market, Toyota increased content and lowered prices in an attempt to combat flagging sales. As mentioned, the Turbo six-speed returned (though only in Sport Roof form), and the upgraded premium sound system became standard on coupe models. Nonturbo Sport Roof models now included leather interior and the top-line AM/FM/ETR/CD sound system. Non-turbo Supras got the Turbo's "basket handle" rear wing, Turbos got polished alloy wheels, and all models received the obligatory "15th Anniversary" badging. Although chassis rigidity was never a noted problem, the Supra's unibody received structural reinforcements for added stiffness, most likely to compensate for a loss of the same on Sport Roof models. The front lower fascia was slightly revised, and the cabin benefited from a bit more sound-deadening material.

Nineteen ninety-eight brought a new engine for the naturally aspirated Supra; while still a 3.0-liter six, it features a VVT-i variable valve timing system for a broader power band and an increase of five horsepower. Nice, but it was only available with an automatic. The Turbo/six-speed combo once again came with a contingency, as it was not sold in California. Most of the equipment upgrades from the 15th Anniversary packaging carried over for Supra's final year.

We've already raved enough about the Supra Turbo's mechanical sophistication and performance. But with that come two penalties: its propensity to be driven hard and perhaps abused and the critical need for religious maintenance. Regular oil changes are not

important to the life of a Supra twin-turbo six: they are critical, as turbo replacements are expensive—and remember, there are two. Enthusiasts recommend switching to synthetic motor oil the minute you buy one, if it hasn't already been done.

The power steering system also needs to be flushed and refilled, not just filled up, as on most other cars. This step is too often missed, resulting in a failed pump, steering rack, or both. Same for the cooling system: this engine generates a lot of heat, and keeping it cool requires regular radiator flushes and hoses that are in top condition. Make sure to keep debris out of the large, grilleless front air intake. The clutch and throw-out bearing are tough but do wear out; expect replacement as early as 70,000 miles if the car has been driven hard. The expansive black plastic dash is prone to cracking, so treat it often with a UV-fighting Protestant. The electrical systems, brakes, rear end, and most of the rest of the car have proven generally trouble free.

Finally, if 320 horsepower isn't enough for you, know that these fourth-gen Supras are well supported by a fervent aftermarket that can supply all manner of engine and suspension hardware to take it a step further. Common are the 400-horsepower Supra Turbos, and some of the more extremely built-up cars put out a genuine 500. Not to mention the assortment of wheels, wings, and other bodywork goodies that are also available. Expect to pay a premium for a low-mileage, well-maintained example, but it's worth it: That car will be cheaper in the long run than a high-mileage "bargain" that needs work.

In spite of the fact that it never sold in big numbers, the Supra, especially in Turbo form, is one of the most impressive performance cars of the mid-1990s. It is fast, handles well, is comfortable, functions well as an everyday car, and to most eyes it's a great looker. Although a lot of money when new, it's a great performance value on the used sports car market.

SPECIFICATIONS (1994 TURBO)

Body style. . . . . Two door, four passenger
Drivetrain layout . . . . Front engine, rear drive
Engine type . . . . Twin-turbocharged DOHC I-6
Displacement, liter/cc 3.0/2,997
Horsepower, hp @ rpm . . . . SAE net 320 @ 5,800
Torque, ft-lb @ rpm . . . . SAE net 315 @ 4,000
Transmission . . . . 6-speed manual
Wheelbase, in. 100.4
Length, in. 177.7
Width, in. 71.3
Height, in. 50.2
Base curb weight, lb 3,550
Suspension, f/r . . . . Upper and lower A-arms/upper A-arm, lateral link
Steering type. . . . . Rack and pinion
Brakes, f/r . . . . Disc/disc

PERFORMANCE

Acceleration, 0–60 mph . . . . 5.3 sec.
Standing quarter
mile, sec/mph 13.7/105.0
Source. . . . . Road & Track

TYPICAL PARTS/REPAIR PRICES

Major tune-up/service. $290
Air filter 25
Shock absorber 117
Catalytic converter(s) 129
Clutch replacement 825

WEBSITES

mkIV.com
supras.com

Chapter 27

FOR
- Taut styling
- Good handling
- Excellent VR6 engine

AGAINST
- No longer available
- Good ones harder to find
- G-lader engine

HOT PICK
1995 Corrado SLC

REPORT CARD

Engine	A-
Transmission	B+
Power/Weight Ratio	B+
Handling	B+
Braking	B+
Ride	B+
Exterior Styling	B+
Interior Styling	B+
Interior Function	B
Cargo Capacity	B
Everyday Usability	B
Reliability	B+
Fit and Finish	A-
Market Availability	B-
Resale Value Potential	B
Fun Factor	B+
Bang for Buck	B
Aftermarket Interest	A-
Club Support	A-

Volkswagen Corrado (1990–1994)

Sporty coupes, or "Hot Hatches" as British enthusiasts tend to call them, are a funny breed. For some reason, they tend to go in and out of favor. They're "in" for a while, then buyers seem to head off toward sport sedans. Then they're in again, only to lose buyership to the sport/utility vehicle market. Whatever—the 1990s spawned many of them, but to understand the notion behind the VW Corrado, you really need to look back to the mid-1970s.

VW took a huge risk in finally usurping the Beetle with the all-new, water-cooled Rabbit/Golf in 1975. One big advantage offered by the front-drive platform was how easily new rear bodywork, of varying

The Corrado's styling is a cross between the boxy, no-nonsense look of the Rabbit/Golf, and something a bit more flamboyant that might come from Japan, Italy, or the United States. And certainly an improvement to the somewhat dowdy Scirocco that it replaced in VW's lineup. This is a 1991 Corrado G60, meaning it's powered by the supercharged four. *Volkswagen*

Many liken the Corrado to the Audi Coupe and Quattro models of the 1980s; a bit blocky, but nicely proportioned, sporty, and uncluttered. *Volkswagen*

Although this car is also a G60 model, it's virtually identical in appearance to the later SLC VR6 Corrados, except for minor detail differences to the fascias, some different wheel offerings, and of course the badging. *Volkswagen*

lengths, could be built on the back. Thus, there were two- and four-door Rabbits, and the sport sedan-ish Jetta that would soon follow. VW also whipped up a sporty, fast/hatchback coupe called the Scirocco. On the whole, it sold well, and was offered in two iterations through 1987; by the time a third-generation, remodeled Scirocco came along, so did a name change.

The new Corrado coupe made its debut in the U.S. market for the 1990 model year. Along with the new name came an innovative powerplant: the supercharged "G-lader" four-cylinder engine; hence the "Corrado G60" model nomenclature. Although nowadays, we're used to high-revving fours that produce up to (and beyond) 200 horsepower using sophisticated engine management tricks, such as variable valve timing. But at the dawn of the 1990s, most 1.8–2.0 liter fours were good for around 120 horsepower. The G-ladder positive displacement supercharger cranked that rating up to a reasonably healthy 158 horses, making it the most powerful VW offered at the time.

This technologically advanced engine came wrapped in a handsomely designed package that still looks outstanding today. Corrados were built by Karmann in Germany, usually to a very high quality standard. Corrado was only offered in coupe form, with your choice of a stick or automatic transmission. Most of the rest of the mechanicals were shared with the second-generation VW Golf—not a bad thing. Most Corrados came reasonably well equipped, including air conditioning, power windows, steering, and brakes; popular options include a sunroof, ABS brakes, leather seating—even factory-installed BBS wheels. The supercharged four-cylinder version was sold in the U.S. market only during 1990 and 1991 (they first started appearing in Europe in 1988/1989).

Volkswagen launched an all-new, and again somewhat innovative, powerplant in the North American

markets for 1992—the VR6. How good was this narrow angle, high-winding, compact V-6 engine? It's still in production today, having become an important element of VW's engine strategy. What makes it a "narrow angle" V-6? All engines that employ a "V" architecture splay the cylinder banks at some angle. Almost all V-8s are inclined at 90 degrees, as this is where an eight-cylinder's engine pulses are in what's called "perfect balance." For a V-6, that "perfect angle" is 60 degrees. However, using an innovative crankshaft design, the angle between the VR6's cylinder heads is a scant 15 degrees. This means the engine can employ a single cylinder head, which takes up a lot less room in an engine bay. VW couldn't build them fast enough, and began slipping them under the hood of its most performance-oriented models, including the Corrado.

The Corrado VR6 enjoys a 20-horsepower advantage (now 178 ponies) over the more complicated, supercharged four. The parasitic power consumption of the s/c is not separate from the 158-horsepower rating. Moreover, the V-6 was considerably smoother and much quieter in operation. The VR6 became available beginning with the 1992 model. Other changes were relatively modest; the hood was reconfigured to accommodate the VR6 engine, the grille was changed, new colors were offered, and VW fiddled around with the switch gear inside a bit. The model was actually called the Corrado SLC, for Sport Luxury Coupe.

This 1993 Corrado SLC can be identified by the standard equipment 15-inch five-spoke Speedline wheels. The 1991 and 1992s had a genuine BBS classic cross-lace design, while the 1990s used a unique 16-spoke BBS model. *Volkswagen*

Many VW experts consider the VR6-powered, SLC Corrado as VW's best sports car of the 1990s. It's probably true, as it finally combined the Corrado's great shape and competent suspension with the VR6 powertrain. This package is also a bit lighter than the third-generation GTI. Note that the unloaded wheels stay well planted even during relatively hard cornering. *Wes Allison photo, courtesy* Motor Trend

While the Corrado's cabin is a bit dated when compared to cars of the later 1990s, it still offers full instrumentation and reasonably sound ergonomics. Materials are a bit hard and plasticky but of reasonably high quality. *Volkswagen*

Take a look at a clean, well-optioned, leather-trimmed Corrado VR6; the SLC label fits well. The VR6-powered Corrado was offered in the North American market from 1992 through 1994, and went away entirely after the 1995 model year, the final other-markets Corrado being dubbed the Corrado Storm. The Storm was extra special in that it packed a 2.9-liter engine, making 190-horsepower, and was the last Corrado model. But it matters little to U.S. buyers, for, as noted, the Storm was not sold here.

While a certain population of Corrado aficionados are attracted to the G60 cars due to its uniqueness as the only factory-supercharged Volkswagen ever offered, it's hard to beat the VR6 model from a driving standpoint: it's quicker, quieter, smoother, and is likely to be both more reliable and less costly to service. Unless you are stuck on the supercharger's novelty value, or find an unbelievably clean example for a larcenous price, we recommend you focus on a VR6 SLC.

No matter which you choose, you'll be pleased with the Corrado's driving characteristics. It is distinctly German, meaning communicative steering, capable brakes, a firm ride, and well-composed handling. The seats are very firm, and that sloping backlight doesn't offer the rear-seat headroom or cargo capacity that you'll find in the taller, square-rigged Golf, but the appearance and the driving experience have held up well. It doesn't look or drive like a 5- or 10-year-old car.

Corrados have proven to be well built and generally reliable, but there are areas to watch for. Make sure to have any Corrado's fuel system carefully inspected, as they can leak and cause an engine compartment fire. The Corrado Club of America also notes that either model can suffer from balky shifting, due to worn linkage or transmission synchros. The optional ABS system can be problematic, sunroof switch or motor failures seem to be common, and the fog light lenses crack due to heat. Timing belt changes should be documented, and as with any front driver, make sure the CV joints and protection boots are in good shape.

The most critical aspect of a G60 car is, of course, the condition of the supercharger itself. These units can wear as quickly as 50,000—or last as long as 100,000—depending on the care they were given (proper warm-up, frequent oil changes). A rebuilt blower is a $1,500–$2,000 ordeal, and needs to be factored into the price of a high-mile car, or one where the supercharger is already on its way out. You can tell if the supercharger is going south if the engine makes a loud whining noise that rises and falls with engine rpm (all blowers make some whirring sound, but it should be smooth and subdued if the supercharger is in good shape). Poor power output and/or excessive smoke output are additional signs.

Because the Corrado shares its basic underpinnings with the Golf, fervent aftermarket support is available. There are many tuner shops, and several magazines, dedicated to high-performance Volkswagens, and it's not difficult to get a Corrado (especially a VR6) to run and handle with any of today's hottest mid-priced sporty coupes.

SPECIFICATIONS (1993 CORRADO SLC)

Body style	Two door, four passenger
Drivetrain layout	Front engine, front drive
Engine type	SOHC V-6
Displacement, liter/cc	2.8/2,979
Horsepower, hp @ rpm	SAE net 178 @ 5,800
Torque, ft-lb @ rpm	SAE net 177 @ 4,200
Transmission	5-speed manual
Wheelbase, in.	97.3
Length, in.	159.4
Width, in.	65.9
Height, in.	51.9
Base curb weight, lb	2,815
Suspension, f/r	MacPherson strut/trailing arm
Steering type	Rack and pinion
Brakes, f/r	Disc/disc

PERFORMANCE

Acceleration, 0–60 mph	6.9 sec.
Standing quarter mile, sec/mph	15.5/91.0
Source	Road & Track

TYPICAL PARTS/REPAIR PRICES

Major tune-up/service	$340
Air filter	12
Shock absorber	51
Catalytic converter(s)	81
Clutch replacement	1,100

WEBSITE

corrado-club.com

Volkswagen Golf GTI (1990–1999)

VW's first-generation, lightweight, rev-happy GTI was one of the original, if not the original, "pocket rockets" of the early 1980s. Why was this boxy little hatchback so quick and so popular? The original European model would putt around town all day, yet eat the autobahn for hours on end; most of that goodness made it to the U.S. version. The letters "GTI" have stood the test of time and have, more often than not, represented the performance enthusiasts' Rabbit/Golf.

It can be argued that the GTI's game—at least its four-cylinder game—peaked with the 2.0L 16-valve cars built from 1990 to 1992, in final "A2" (internally designated as the "A" platform, second-generation)

Many feel that the last of the second-generation Golf platform represents the GTI in its purest form. They have more power and a better chassis than the very earliest GTIs, yet don't carry the complication and weight of the extra luxury features that showed up in the 1993–1996 machines. This is a 1991 model; note the Euro-style driving lights built into the grille. *Volkswagen*

An exceptional GTI if you can find one, this being a last-of-the-Mark II-model 1992 GTI 16V, packing the higher-output four-valve-per-cylinder head and more horsepower. The car in this factory press photo features the coveted two-piece 15-inch BBS wheels, and low-profile tires that came with it were standard equipment on only the 1990–1992 2.0-liter 16V GTIs. *Volkswagen*

form. The early Rabbit-based cars achieved lightness by sacrificing some structural rigidity and offering more rudimentary interiors, with the exception of their oft-stolen Recaro seats. Later A3-bodied GTIs were heavier and lacked the flickable, nimble handling that was the model's primary stock in trade. So the last of these A2 cars arguably stand as a bit of a high water-mark, even though it was on the 1995 A3 version that we first got to sample the wonderful VR6.

As noted, A2 Golfs are relatively lightweight, our chosen source indicating a 2,450-pound curb weight at the high end, while being significantly more rigid than the original Rabbit GTI, and with improved rear suspension and the addition of four-wheel disc brakes. The 1.8-liter 16V Volkswagen developed 123 horsepower for the U.S. market; this, combined with the GTI's lightness, ensured nothing else in the category could run with it.

When the change was made to the 2.0L Passat block in 1990 (this book's real starting point), output increased to 134 horsepower, but with a 6.4-millimeter longer stroke, midrange torque was improved even more, the peak of 120 ft-lb at 4,250 rpm growing to 133 ft-lb at 4,400 rpm. At the same time, the engine management finally was updated to a modern, fully computer-controlled system, but the fuel distibutor and injectors were still mechanical. Although Japanese manufacturers have surpassed the 16V Volkswagen in output and, yes, smoothness, the VW has a raspy, playful, born-to-run character, closer in spirit to an old Alfa Romeo GTV than to the smoother, 8,000-rpm high-winders found in the Japanese brands, particularly Honda and Acura.

The GTI was also offered during these years with a two-valve-per-cylinder engine (8V) rated at 102

horsepower; while these cars handle just as well as the 16V models, it's worth seeking out a 16V car for its extra 31 horsepower.

Like any modern engine machined from quality materials to close tolerances, a properly maintained 16V Volkswagen will run nearly forever. The 2.0L 16V does have a few peripheral components that tend to go bad. Front motor mounts should almost be considered a consumable on these cars. Emissions equipment,

The factory-offered Recaro sport seats in this 1990 Wolfsburg Edition GTI offered outstanding side support and grip due to the thick bolsters and ribbed fabric. This certainly helps keep the driver and passenger in place during hard cornering maneuvers—if you can keep the seats in place in the car. Many a thief will steal a GTI just for its Recaro seats and BBS wheels, then abandon the car. *Volkswagen*

Enthusiasts are divided on the third-generation Golf GTI sold between 1993 and 1998. Some feel that it represented a worthy upgrade, due to its structurally stiffer chassis, higher feature and safety content, and the availability of the wonderful VR6 engine. The truth is somewhere in the middle: the four-cylinder GTIs of this era offer the least performance of any GTI, and are best avoided unless you plan to spend some serious money in the Volkswagen aftermarket. *Volkswagen*

such as the exhaust gas recirculation system or the catalytic converter, sometimes needs attention. Knock sensor wiring can be troublesome, and older spark plug wires may crack and arc to the cylinder head, causing misfires and rough running. The expert we quizzed estimated that 70 percent or more of the 16V cars he sees leak oil into the distributor cap, again causing rough running. This is an easy item to check, simply by removing the distributor cap. The culprit is a simple seal that is not available separately from Volkswagen. Instead, the distributor must be replaced, a tab of $200–$250. Drive axle CV boots should be checked visually. If they are intact, the joints should be fine. If they are torn or cracked, the joints either make noise or will soon, and require replacement. Quality remanufactured axles are available reasonably.

The two biggest liabilities can be addressed with preventive maintenance. The VW 16V is an interference or "contact" design, meaning if the timing belt breaks, the valves and pistons will make a determined attempt to occupy the same space (contact!). Repairs will cost thousands of dollars, possibly even requiring replacement of the head. Volkswagen recommends 60,000-mile timing belt changes, but an

expert suggested that changing the belt and tensioner at 45,000 miles, for a tab of a little under $200, is cheap insurance.

The last potentially large trouble spot is in the transmission. The ring gear is riveted to the differential, and the rivets tend to crack and come out. It is then only a matter of time until this piece of hardened steel causes the demise of the transmission. Most owners ignore any signs, although it's difficult to detect the fault before serious damage has already been done. Grinding noises, sudden and severe shifting problems, or simply locking up without warning are the usual indications. Complete replacement of the transmission is generally required. If you elect to have the damaged transmission overhauled, make sure that all reused parts are magnafluxed for soundness. Unfortunately, there was no recall for this problem, as it tends not to occur until higher mileages. Preventive maintenance is by far the wise choice, and consists simply of replacing the rivets with a Volkswagen-offered bolt kit and installing two C-clips. Labor costs far exceed parts costs, but going through the whole transmission and replacing any worn bearings or synchros at the same time makes the service a reasonable investment on

If you have the money for a 1998 or 1999, well, why not spend a bit more and get the fourth-generation car, with its many updates and exceptional handling prowess. However, a clean 1996 VR6, as shown here, is old enough to be a great buy. *Volkswagen*

these older GTIs if you expect to hang onto the car for the long term.

The MKIII Golf, replacing the previous generation in 1993, didn't receive an engine really worthy of powering a GTI until the top-shelf Corrado SLC was phased out in 1995. From 1992 to 1995, the Corrado had been the sporty hatchback showcasing one of Volkswagen's greatest technical coups, the VR6 engine; the GTI finally got it just as the Corrado went away.

By using only a 15-degree vee and a single-cylinder head, a 2.8L V6 engine fit in the space of a four cylinder. It brought entry-level luxury credentials to Volkswagen, accenting the lineup's separation from its four-cylinder rivals with power, smoothness, and a sweet, sweet sound. The third iteration of the Golf continued to grow up, getting heavier as it became larger and more luxurious. Little was changed fundamentally about the chassis, it was just stronger and more durable, with generally superior design and execution of details. The Passat's passive steering arrangement was adopted for the twist-beam rear suspension, as on the Corrado, but most other mechanical changes were related to emissions control, OBD, and other developments in electronics.

Although four-cylinder Volkswagens have been shown to handle better than VR6 cars, thanks to a smaller chunk of cast iron overhanging the front wheels, that doesn't stop a determined and skilled driver with a VR6 from embarrassing the air-cooled

The third-generation GTi interior is typically Germanic in nature, very clean if a bit plasticky, but all controls are easy to see and reach. Everything operates with a crisp action, and well-bolstered, nicely trimmed leather seats are comfy and supportive. This is a 1996 GTI VR6.

crowd at Porsche club events, and most enthusiasts agree that the VR6 is the only MKIII car to consider for factory performance. The 2.0L crossflow eight-valve GTI set a low watermark for Volkswagen, slower than the original 1983 GTI and, some say, unworthy of the trademarked letters.

VR6-powered cars have fewer liabilities than the 16V GTI. The plastic thermostat housing tends to crack and should be changed at 80,000 miles, and water pumps usually go bad around the century mark. A secondary electric water pump on the side of the head above the tranny may also fail. Coolant leaks in this area indicate trouble. The VR6 drives its cams with a chain, which should require no attention. Transmissions are likely in good shape if there is no grinding on a 1-2 upshift, but a worn second-gear synchro is common. As with the earlier cars, drive-axle CV boots should be checked and replaced if torn.

Volkswagen introduced the concept of fwd performance to the U.S. market with the original GTI in 1983, an economy car that was faster than a contemporary Z28 Camaro, and laid the groundwork for the current import craze. They still offer a certain satisfaction and feel that seems to come only from a German car, and make practical everyday transportation to boot.

SPECIFICATIONS (1996 GTI VR6)

Body style	Two door, five passenger
Drivetrain layout	Front engine, front drive
Engine type	DOHC I-4
Displacement, liter/cc	2.8/2,792
Horsepower, hp @ rpm	SAE net 172 @ 5,800
Torque, ft-lb @ rpm	SAE net 173 @ 4,200
Transmission	5-speed manual
Wheelbase, in.	97.4
Length, in.	160.4
Width, in.	66.7
Height, in.	56.2
Base curb weight, lb	2,765
Suspension, f/r	MacPherson strut/beam axle w/trailing arm
Steering type	Rack and pinion
Brakes, f/r	Disc/disc

PERFORMANCE

Acceleration, 0–60 mph	7.2 sec.
Standing quarter mile, sec/mph	15.6/91.5
Source	Road & Track

TYPICAL PARTS/REPAIR PRICES

Shock absorber	$282
Wheel	12
Fender	53
Headlight	124
Clutch replacement	800

WEBSITES

gti.sfu.org
vwworld.com

Index

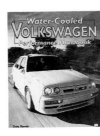

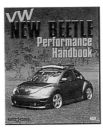